PULSE OF THE MARKET

PULSE OF THE MARKET

MAKING MONEY AND AVOIDING MISTAKES

Malcolm Kaufman

ISBN: 1523952741
ISBN 13: 9781523952748

Preface

AT&T Park's opening in March 2000 helped ignite a wave of condominium-building construction south of Market Street.

I knew nothing about this part of San Francisco, so I decided to do some research in an effort to educate my clients and myself. This effort turned into my writing a monthly newsletter, *Pulse of the Market,* which became a way for me to keep in touch with clients and to help educate them.

This book contains *Pulses* from 2005 to 2015, a ten-year period that includes a wave of robust condominium development followed by the great recession, which was followed by another wave of development that is still underway.

The book is divided into four sections:

- the drivers that underpin the San Francisco residential market
- the neighborhoods that have taken shape in the last ten or more years

- major condominium buildings that have sprung up in these neighborhoods
- insights, perspectives, and other issues

Malcolm Kaufman

What You Should Know about
San Francisco Residential Real Estate

TABLE OF CONTENTS

CHAPTER 1

THE MARKET

These *Pulses* cover the years between 2005 and 2015, a period that includes two up cycles of robust appreciation and the great recession

This chapter is about what drives the San Francisco market. San Francisco is a very special (expensive) market. There are multiple drivers that underpin the long-term upward trend, and it makes little sense to try to "time the market," whether one is buying or selling.

The economy and the real estate market are cyclical. Short-term cycles come and go. It is the long-term cycles that matter. Keep that in mind, for that is where the money is.

The Soufflé Has Arrived
October 2005

Is It a Good Time to Buy or Sell?

This is the constant question I get from prospective clients. I say "prospective clients" because my buyers have already made the decision to buy, and my sellers have made the decision to sell.

Real buyers buy because they're new to the city, or they're financially ready to make the transition from renter to owner, a good thing to do in any market. Sellers typically sell because of a job relocation, the need for more or less space, a death, or a divorce.

I tell my clients that it's a good time to buy if they plan to be in San Francisco for at least three to five years. Even if you bought a condominium at the top of the market in 2000, the odds are pretty good that you've done well financially, especially if you purchased a single-family home.

While the psychological effects of Katrina are likely to pass in short order, the climb in interest rates is an incremental cost that will stay with us (until interest rates go down again). In checking with one of my preferred mortgage brokers, I learned that the five-year ARM is now 5.75 percent versus 5.25 percent just six months ago. Every increase in interest rates is bound to impact a segment of the buying public, which in turn will decrease the number of buyers and have a moderating effect on selling prices.

The question of whether it's a good time to buy or sell is really a question of commitment. How important is it to you personally? What is at stake?

So if you really want to know if it's a good time to buy San Francisco real estate, pay attention to the data and trends, but evaluate them within the context of your needs. After all, it's always a good time to buy and sell for someone. The question is, what's good for you?

Who's Going to Buy All Those Units? February 2007

There Is a Lot of Money Floating Around

Last week I met with a client who heads up the San Francisco wealth-management business for one of the country's major banks. He mentioned that his shop was inundated with unprecedented amounts of money.

Guess Who Has It?

A "boomer" is an American born between 1946 and 1964. There are 76,957,164 boomers (about 26.7 percent of the total US population).

Of course, not all boomers are wealthy, but my guess is that at least the top 1 percent of them (about 769,000) most likely are. With California representing more than 10 percent of the nation's population, I figure that there are probably seven million or more boomers and that there are 75,000 or more high-end boomers living with you, Governor Arnold, and me here in California. Add to that number the Googlers and others who have made millions at a younger age than the boomers did, not to mention the wealthy overseas who are attracted to the economic engine and political stability of the United States, and we get a pretty large number of people supporting the demand side of San Francisco residential real estate.

Reurbanization

My question is, when the boomers retire and their nests empty, what will happen next? Will they move to sunnier climes as their parents did before them, or will they choose to be in an urban area, where they'll be able to enjoy dining, entertainment, and shopping—and forget about commuting?

I think a good number of them will move into the city, and while they may initially keep their primary residence in the South Bay, East Bay, or Marin, ultimately, they will likely make San Francisco their primary home.

About ten years ago, when I was still living in Los Angeles, I was in my car listening to a report from the head of the transportation authority for Orange County. He said, "However bad your commute was today, it is the best that is going to be for the rest of your life." OMG!

Summing Up

Soaring construction costs notwithstanding, I bet that most of the planned condominiums will eventually be built. And while demand may ebb from time to time as psychology changes, there are nonetheless multiple demand drivers that will support the construction boom over the next ten or more years.

We enjoy basic demand from population growth, company expansions, and new family formations. And we also have the big boomer wave, empty nesting, the rise of commute-phobia, and enormous pools of money looking for a safe investment in a prime location.

Quality Wins Out
April 2008

A friend of mine sent me a client newsletter from an investment manager. I would like to share a few paragraphs of it:

> We don't invest based on expectations of what the market will do next month or even next quarter. We invest based on expectations about future earnings and cash flows, factors that reflect the real value of a company beyond the short-term emotion-driven ebbs and flows of the market.
>
> Trying to time the market for possible short-term advantages is inconsistent with a focused strategy designed for the long haul where selecting **quality** stocks becomes the crucial variable.
>
> In the last 12 months ending January, producer prices climbed the largest increase since October 1981. In the future, companies will be forced to more fully pass these costs along to consumers. In simple English, this means that you can expect higher prices for almost everything; it is going to **cost** you more to live in the future.

As I read the above, two words jumped out at me: cost and quality.

Cost

It's expensive to live in San Francisco; it always has been, and it's not going to get any cheaper. Not everyone gets the message. Some of my clients are actually waiting for prices to fall, convinced that real estate in San Francisco will crash just like it did in the rest of the country.

I can't cite statistics for the last few years' increased cost of basic residential building materials—concrete, steel, and copper—or for the costs of labor and soft development costs.

However, I haven't met a developer who hasn't bemoaned the rapid rise in all of those prices. I recall talking with a major developer in 2005, when his firm was getting ready to excavate for a new high-rise residential tower. The original budget for the cost to build was $450 per square foot. As the building neared completion, the new reality looked more like $650 per square foot. I'm not sure where that price ended up, but I would bet that it exceeded $650 per square foot. Today it would probably be north of $800 per square foot!

It's going to be more expensive in the future!

Another issue is that the land is getting scarcer and more costly, whether it is in the Financial District, South Beach, SOMA, or Mission Bay. The availability of parking lots is diminishing.

So while some people develop heart palpitations as new-condo sale prices near $1,000 per square foot, they will no doubt have a total coronary when homes approach $1,500 per square foot. For those who wish to avoid heart medicine, I recommend Tulsa, Oklahoma, where there are good steaks, and you don't have to make excuses for the Giants or 49ers.

Quality

The above investment manager focused on quality companies—that is, those with fundamentally sound balance sheets and quality earnings. So it goes with real estate. When it comes to single-family homes, buyers want to live in the better neighborhoods in a quality home. Progression and regression are two basic concepts that persist in the residential real estate industry. Simply stated, "progression" is when the better homes on a block typically raise the value of the lesser homes, while "regression" refers to the tendency of a neighborhood of low-value homes to pull down the value of the more expensive homes.

Buyers would rather buy and own the least expensive home on a block of expensive, higher-quality homes than the most expensive home on a block of inexpensive or average-quality homes.

The same thing holds true with high-rise buildings in the south of Market neighborhoods. The quality of the buildings is determined by their location and amenities. I would much rather own a lesser unit in a quality building than an expensive unit in a lower-quality building. In the long term, as with the stock market, quality will win out.

Here's the bottom line: each building has a value that either adds to or subtracts from the value of an individual unit.

Summing Up

Like the stock market, the emotions of residential buyers and sellers ebb and flow. Right now, some buyers are concerned about the credit markets or their jobs. Unlike in most other cities in the country, San Francisco residential demand is supported by multiple buyer categories—those who want a primary residence because they work here, empty nesters, pied-à-terre buyers, investors, and "home collectors" who are wealthy and comfortable with placing some of their assets in the San Francisco real estate market. When one or two categories weaken, the others support demand.

A 9.0 Worldwide Earthquake October 2008

Folks, we just had the equivalent of a 9.0 financial earthquake, this one with an epicenter in New York City and London, and it was all man made. The aftershocks are being felt throughout the world, and there will be aftershocks aplenty!

Yes, we are going to feel the effects—probably for some time—of the financial earthquake. But I would rather be here than in New York, where the financial community represents a much bigger piece of the economic pie; in a city like Detroit, which was already experiencing hard times; or in the many smaller communities just twenty-five miles or so outside of San Francisco, where subprime and Alt-A loans have run wild.

Perspective

I get that people are scared and maybe in shock, but *not everyone* is. I did an informal survey among real estate agents last week. I asked two questions: Do you perceive a slowdown in traffic for resales, and do you perceive a greater hesitancy on the part of buyers? An overwhelming majority of those who answered said yes to both questions—but not all did. One agent characterized the traffic situation as "slightly less traffic for B properties and strong traffic for A properties," meaning that *some buyers* feel that it is currently the time to get a great deal.

My sense is that between 80 and 90 percent of buyers are not going to do anything for a while. I also sense that between 10 and 20 percent will take action based on a real need to buy, either because they've made a commitment to relocate to the city for a new job or are empty nesters and have already made a decision to move. Remember, as the Dow Jones plummets some three or four hundred points on any given day, there is always a buyer on the other side of each trade

Bright Spots

Buying residential real estate is not a short-term trade. One needs a five-to-seven-year horizon. If we review average San Francisco prices for both single-family homes and condominiums for the last twenty years, we'll see that regardless of the year you bought in, you would have experienced appreciation over the ensuing five to seven years

Take, for example, the area south of Market Street, where some would say excessive building has taken place over the last few years. The good news for recent buyers is that their property value is probably going to rise simply because there's going to be less construction in the next three to five years. Some projects will be canceled outright, while others will be delayed. Lenders are going to sit on their money until their collective confidence and capital are renewed. Also, the cost of construction is up significantly, and there probably won't be any significant projects built until the financial situation stabilizes *and* sales prices go up. The fact that there are fewer condominiums for sale, even in the face of lesser demand, bodes well for today's owner or buyer. And the fact that (the majority of) sellers are also nervous means that attractive deals are to be had in this troubled market.

THE MARKET FEELS SQUISHY! JUNE 2010

"The market feels squishy" was a comment from a client who had been in negotiation to buy a condominium at one of the Seven Sisters. She had returned from a holiday in Italy and had flown back the evening before the Dow took a 376-point dive (on top of a 1,000-point plunge two weeks earlier) and was a bit jet-lagged.

My question is, would you rather buy stock in Apple after a 25-point jump or after a 25-point plunge? The market probably feels pretty squishy after a 25-point plunge; you're still buying stock in the same company, though. It's tough to pull the trigger in a squishy market. Nevertheless, that is when the best deals are made

So Why Buy Now?

There's a dwindling inventory: There are fewer new products on the market than there were one or two years ago. The Infinity managed to sell 300 or more units in 2009. In February 2010 they had 20 or more units available. Now they are down to 2—out of 650!

Both One Rincon Hill and the Millennium are pretty closed mouth, but my G-2 tells me that they've been making good sales progress in 2010.

SOMA Grand, Arterra, the Hayes, One South Park, Park Terrace, and Radiance are all sold out.

There's new inventory: One Hawthorne, a new 165-unit development, came to market in April. It's too early to tell how it's faring. It should do ok because it's well located and the sole development to open its doors this year.

I don't know of any other major development that's had or will have a chance of breaking ground during the next twelve months. Maybe Radiance Two in Mission Bay will break ground toward the end of 2010.

Before we get more inventory, prices need to rise to justify new construction, and lenders need to be convinced that a development can sell out in a reasonable time.

A Seven Sisters–quality building with underground parking and an off-site, affordable housing element would probably cost $700 or more per square foot to build and would require an average of $900 or more per square foot to pencil.

There is high demand: San Francisco has a population of fewer than 800,000 people, and there are many renters who would like to be homeowners. Demand also comes from the seven million or more Bay Area souls who live in surrounding counties, a number of whom are drawn to the city by the sirens of dining or entertainment and end up buying. And when the kiddies are gone and these folks are no longer willing to travel the freeways, they may downsize and buy in San Francisco.

Meaning?

While the market may feel squishy to my client, what she is really saying is that the future is not certain enough for her to feel confident about making a major financial commitment. No one said this is easy.

Fear or Not
September 2010

I cherish my Saturday mornings with my coffee, bagel, *New York Times,* and *Wall Street Journal.* I usually start with the *Times,* as I did a couple of Saturdays ago. When I got to the business section, two articles presented themselves to me.

I first read Ron Lieber's "In Defense of Home Ownership." It begins, "It's hard to read the headlines and not conclude that becoming a homeowner is a terrible idea." And then notes that "millions of home-owners are still far underwater [and] the conventional wisdom says that home values will never again rise faster than inflation."

After laying this groundwork, he talks about specific couples and their reasonable approaches to buying in this market. I found his article to be very sound and refreshing. I recommend it to you.

Also on the first business page was Joe Nocera's "Widespread Fear Freezes Housing Market." With a title like that, would anyone actually read the article? Fortified with a second cup of coffee, I jumped in. Here are a few of his comments:

1. "You have to wonder sometimes what they're smoking over there at the National Association of Realtors."
2. "The Realtors group reported that it now takes more than a year to sell a typical house."

3. "For months, the Obama tax credit had been the only grease in the housing market. Now that it is gone, the buying and selling of houses is essentially grinding to a halt."
4. "Essentially, every participant in the housing market has a reason to be afraid. And that fear is paralyzing."
5. "There is an immense amount of inventory that has yet to hit the market."

If I were Mr. or Ms. Consumer and thinking about buying or selling but had read Joe Nocera's article first, I would certainly reach for whatever they're smoking over at the National Association of Realtors. It has to be less of a hallucinogen than what Nocera is smoking. Any time you put the word "fear" in a headline, you are going to spur readership, which, as we all know, sells newspapers

The two articles differ in tone but also in basic ideas. Nocera talks about dire national statistics and draws inferences to make his points. Lieber, on the other hand, is telling a specific story of couples shopping for a home and discusses why they're doing so amid the current challenged economic environment.

I'm sure that there are real estate markets in this country that are every bit as bad as Nocera is saying. However, we are in San Francisco, and I'm here to tell you that even though it's not all peaches and cream, deals—and good deals—are being made. Here are my answers to Nocera:

1. We already talked about smoking.
2. I listed a $1 million condominium in Noe Valley in mid-August, which, according to conventional wisdom, is the wrong time since everyone (except me) is on vacation. We

went into contract at full price in eight days, not the "more than a year [required] to sell a typical house."

3. The buyer got a thirty-year mortgage through Wells Fargo at 5.15 percent. It seems that there is plenty of grease over at Wells.
4. I had sixty people for the first Sunday open and had fifty or more agents through on the first brokers' tour. They were walking and talking, and if they were paralyzed, it was not noticeable.
5. I wonder how Nocera knows that there is an immense amount of inventory that has yet to hit the market. In making that statement, he is doing nothing more than repeating what others in the press have been speculating for more than a year. It's a fear tactic meant to grab eyeballs and concomitantly strike fear into the hearts of readers. Bull puppy!

Feel Good and Feel Bad
April 2011

Here's my conundrum. In the last few weeks, I have read a number of articles on the 2010 census. I also finished reading Richard Florida's *Who's Your City?*, which I highly recommend. I feel good about the future of San Francisco real estate, but I feel bad for many of the folks in other parts of the country.

From the 2010 Census

Detroit is now the poorest city in the United States, and it has a 50 percent unemployment rate. In 1947, it had 3,272 manufacturing firms that employed 338,400 workers. In 1972, it had 1,518 manufacturing firms that employed 180,400 workers. Other industrial cities—like Cleveland, Chicago, Cincinnati, Toledo, Pittsburgh, Saint Louis, and Buffalo—have all experienced significant manufacturing and population declines.

While the census is all about population composition and trends, real estate appreciation is based on factors other than population growth, according to Florida's book.

The following table speaks volumes.

Real annualized house appreciation, 1950–2000
Top and bottom ten metro areas with 1950 population > 500,000

Top Ten MSAs by Price Growth Annualized growth rate 1950-2000		Bottom Ten MSAs by Price Growth Annualized growth rate 1950-2000	
San Francisco*	3.53	San Antonio	1.13
Oakland	2.82	Milwaukee	1.06
Seattle	2.74	Pittsburgh	1.02
San Diego	2.61	Dayton	0.99
Los Angeles	2.46	Albany, NY	0.97
Portland	2.36	Cleveland	0.91
Boston	2.30	Rochester, NY	0.89
Bergen-Passaic, NJ	2.19	Youngstown-Warren	0.81
Charlotte	2.18	Syracuse	0.67
New Haven	2.12	Buffalo	0.54

Note: Average = 1.70

*The rates are for the San Francisco *metro area*, which comprises nine Bay Area counties and not just the city of San Francisco itself.

Source: Joseph Gyourko, Christopher Mayer, and Todd Sinai

The six cities with the highest appreciation are all on the West Coast, except for San Antonio. The lowest-growth cities are former centers of the industrial age.

Superstar Cities

The "superstar" cities listed above did not reach this level because of greater population growth. According to University of Pennsylvania professor Joseph Gyourko, in the short term, real estate prices in superstar cities experience significant ups and downs, but over time they consistently appreciate in value. They are, according to Gyourko, "by their nature exclusionary—and due to the prices they command, residents have to pay a significant financial premium to live there."

The following map by Ryan Morris is interesting. If you want to be in the entertainment industry, for example, you will most likely move to Los Angeles; if you want to be in the aerospace industry, to the Seattle area; and if you want to be in the wine-making industry, to Napa.

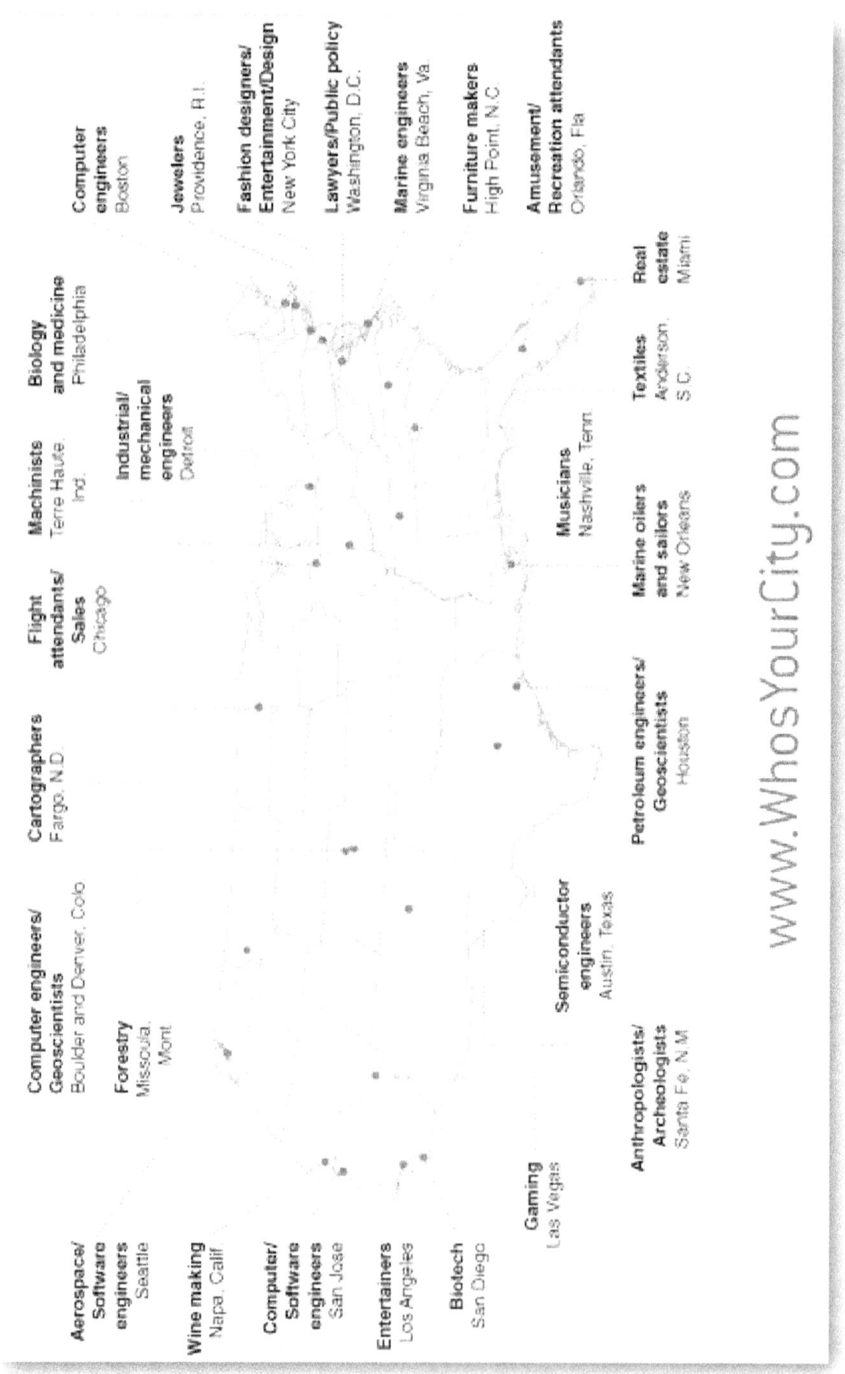
Aerospace/ Software engineers
Seattle
Wine making
Napa, Calif
Computer/ Software engineers
San Jose
Entertainers
Los Angeles
Biotech
San Diego
Gaming
Las Vegas
Computer engineers/ Geoscientists
Boulder and Denver, Colo
Forestry
Missoula, Mont
Anthropologists/ Archeologists
Santa Fe, N.M
Semiconductor engineers
Austin, Texas
Cartographers
Fargo, N.D.
Petroleum engineers/ Geoscientists
Houston
Flight attendants/ Sales
Chicago
Marine oilers and sailors
New Orleans
Machinists
Terre Haute, Ind.
Musicians
Nashville, Tenn.
Industrial/ mechanical engineers
Detroit
Textiles
Anderson, S.C.
Biology and medicine
Philadelphia
Real estate
Miami
Computer engineers
Boston
Jewelers
Providence, R.I.
Fashion designers/ Entertainment/Design
New York City
Lawyers/Public policy
Washington, D.C.
Marine engineers
Virginia Beach, Va.
Furniture makers
High Point, N.C.
Amusement/ Recreation attendants
Orlando, Fla
www.WhosYourCity.com

Superstar cities act as a natural filter for residents who expect to see high returns on their education and skill sets. The premium prices are not only related to areas of limited supply and strict zoning rules but also to the fact that talented/educated people want to interact with other talented/educated people. In addition, artists and bohemians not only produce amenities but also are attracted to places that have them.

In effect, there is a snowball effect of talent attraction. The talented/educated workforce is clustering around a few major urban areas. I personally hope that the U.S. car manufacturers get back on their feet and that Detroit is able to pull out of its nose dive. A small number of major metropolitan areas are attracting the lion's share of the highly skilled and highly educated. A larger question is whether we want everyone in our major metro area to be roughly as well off and as skilled as we are.

New York Has Russians—
We Have Our Own
April 2012

What do Dmitry Rybolovlev, Igor Krutoy, and Andrei Vavilov have in common with Mark Zuckerberg, Mark Pincus, and Reid Hoffman? If the first three are not familiar to you, allow me to introduce them.

Dmitry Rybolovlev, a trained physician and one of Russia's first stockbrokers, became the chairman of Uralkali at the age of twenty-nine in 1996. In 2000, it was valued at $15 million. It went public in 2007, and by 2008 it was valued at $34 billion.

Igor Krutoy learned how to play the accordion as a child and then went on to write over one hundred popular songs in Russia and to collaborate with virtually every major Russian music star. He has released over thirty albums and has sold over twenty million records. He organized the first music channel in Russia and owns his own record company, ARS, and radio station, Love Radio.

Andrei Vavilov is a Russian politician, businessman, and senator, and he is a former first-deputy finance minister of Russia. He holds a PhD in economics. He arranged the issue of the first Russian Eurobonds on the international market.

What do these three Russians have in common? They have each spent an average of $50 million for a Manhattan penthouse condominium, paying more than $4,000 per square foot and, in the process, resetting the price point of the high-end real estate market in New York.

The Few versus the Many

While a few Russians are setting the bar for the very high end in New York, they are only a few. Rather than a few Russians, here in San Francisco and the Peninsula, there are many companies and people doing the same thing. They are the recipients of stock options at many levels throughout the many companies that call the Bay Area home, including Google, OpenTable, Yelp, Pandora, Salesforce, Tesla, Zynga, LinkedIn, Facebook, Airbnb, AKQA, Dropbox, Eventbrite, Kabam, Kixeye, Splunk, Square, Trulia, Twitter, and Yammer.

Wealth Creation

Much of the wealth creation in Russia over the last two decades resulted from the privatization of Russia's basic industries. Here the wealth is being created through technological innovation.

Let's Wait—or Not
September 2012

Here are two overheard conversations.

The first conversation was about three reasons to buy now and to not wait:

1. We need more room—the baby is coming!
2. We just sold our home in _____ (Alamo, Ross, or any other city—just fill in the blank).
3. I am relocating to San Francisco for a new job.

The second conversation was about three reasons to wait:

1. Let's see what happens in the election.
2. The fiscal cliff may make a difference.
3. I don't see prices rising.

For the first group, their events are game changers. Each demands a decision; time is not a friend. The second group can dither all it wants.

Courage

It takes courage to make a decision. I keep thinking back to October 2001, when a client made a courageous decision to buy a condominium right after September 11. The real estate market was frozen. My client chose to act, and he made an attractive deal because he had the courage to pull the trigger in the face of a confused market. He was thinking long term and took advantage of short-term market uncertainty.

Hey, there is always short-term uncertainty in the marketplace! My favorite buyer clients are the ones who are having the first conversation. Those who are engaged in the second conversation need not apply. My favorite seller clients are the ones who are also thinking long term and have a reason to sell now.

The nuances of the election, the fiscal cliff, and the unstable Euro are not going to matter in five years. Where you want to live in five years does matter.

How 'Bout Those Giants! November 2012

Exactly two years ago, after the Giants won the World Series, I wrote a *Pulse of the Market* using an American dream metaphor that linked the Giants' winning with owning a home:

As kids, we dream of standing at the plate and making a hit that scores the winning run. As adults, we dream of owning our own home. Both are symbols of the American dream.

I liken winning the World Series to a once-in-a-lifetime experience like buying the home of your dreams.

Detroit

This past week, I read an article written by Edward Glaeser, an economics professor at Harvard. I urge you to read "Why San Francisco Beat Detroit" to appreciate San Francisco's triumph over Detroit on a deeper level.

Glaeser talks about the entrepreneurial ethos of San Francisco. While entrepreneurship may not be directly linked to baseball, the concept does suggest something about the long term viability of San Francisco's real estate.

We are a city of creative ideas and great educational institutions. Both are key reasons why people want to live here, not to mention the physical and environmental beauty.

Two years ago, when we won the Series, San Francisco was still in the real estate doldrums. Today there are clear signs that prices are recovering. In fact, average prices through October 2012 are up more than 10 percent over 2011.

I concluded my November 2010 *Pulse* by saying, "Yes, I hear all the talk about [how] it makes more economic sense to rent than to buy (ok as an interim solution, but not a good long term strategy), prices are still going down, [and] unemployment is still going up."

You cannot turn a property you rent into the home of your dreams; nor can you leave it to your kids. More importantly, your home is an asset that will likely appreciate and contribute to wealth.

Good Giant players are a limited resource. Land is certainly a limited resource here in San Francisco, though it's not in Detroit. Stick with the dream.

Good for Sellers and Bad for Buyers February 2013

Last February's *Pulse of the Market,* "Have We Hit Bottom?" posited that the San Francisco residential market had hit bottom. Results for 2012 confirm that.

Where Do We Go from Here?

The next five years will be good for sellers and bad for buyers. San Francisco is on the cusp of another (strong) leg up in residential prices.

Jones Lang LaSalle, a major commercial real estate company, held an event on January 30 at which it forecast a strong outlook for the city. A few items caught my attention:

> Boston Properties is so bullish on the future of San Francisco that it is investing more than twice as much capital in the city's office market as it is in the rest of the country combined. (Editor's note: WOW!)
>
> San Francisco is among the top seven cities worldwide benefiting from the three forces of urbanization, globalization, and modernization.

> San Francisco has more than three times the tech start-ups as London and four times the number in New York City.
>
> The CEO of Rocket Space, a shared work space company, said he was inundated with calls from companies worldwide looking to get a window into the San Francisco market. "We get twenty-five applications a week from companies all over the world wanting to put small teams here. These are large multinational companies, and they want an innovation team in San Francisco of ten to fifteen people."

For each new software designer hired by Twitter in San Francisco, there are five new job openings for baristas, personal trainers, doctors, and taxi drivers. Most sectors have a multiplier effect, but the innovation sector has the largest multiplier effect of all—it's about three times larger than that of the manufacturing industry.

How Long and How Much?
May 2013

How long will this up cycle last, and how much appreciation will there be? These are the questions for this *Pulse.* I'm estimating that it will last for five to seven years and that there will be an average of 10 percent appreciation per year during the current cycle. In other words, we are in the second inning of a five- or seven-inning ball game. Holy cow!

Recent History

I have condominium and single-family-home average sales data back only to 1994—the MLS numbers are sketchy at best before then. The year 1994 was the start of an up cycle that lasted for seven years and ended in 2000 with a decline that most of us remember. During that up cycle, both single-family homes and condominiums appreciated a total of 90 or more percent for the entire period, or more than 13 percent a year.

The market then faltered and started another up cycle in 2003/2004, and there was appreciation of more than 40 percent with an average of 8 percent per year until the peak in 2007/2008. We then suffered a decline in average prices of 15 to 20 percent during the great recession, which bottomed out in 2011.

We saw prices rise dramatically in 2012, during which there was an average price increase of 16.6 percent for single-family homes and 11.4 percent for condominiums. Where do we go from here?

Market Drivers

This market is being propelled on a number of fronts. The drivers include a lack of inventory, a lack of new construction, low interest rates, Asian buyers looking for a safe place to park some cash, low unemployment (now about 6 percent), healthier state and city budgets, a nexus with Silicon Valley, and the recognition that San Francisco is a special *innovation hub* that attracts companies and employees.

These drivers will eventually change, and some of them may peter out, but change will take time. Because the most recent recession was so dramatic, my sense is that the current bounce will be unusually strong and will last for five to seven years. No one really knows, but I am willing to go out on a limb and state an opinion. It helps to have an opinion about the future when making decisions about the present.

FIVE THINGS YOU MAY WANT TO KNOW JUNE 2013

The New Geography of Jobs by Enrico Moretti is a must-read book. It explains why San Francisco is one of the world's most important innovation hubs and what that means for you and me as owners or renters.

Two

What happens in Silicon Valley impacts San Francisco. Google, Nvidia, Samsung, Facebook, and Apple are all building new one-million-or-more-square-foot campuses. Ergo, there is great demand for construction labor and materials, which is driving up the prices of new commercial and residential construction here in the city.

Three

There are only a few major condominium developments coming soon. Tishman Speyer's Infinity Two complex (655 units at 201 Folsom) will break ground later in June. Millennium Partners appears to be winning its battle to build a forty-seven-story tower with 215 units at 706 Mission (at Third Street); it will include a four-story Mexican Museum. Bosa Development is getting ready to start a new development at block 12 East along Mission Creek that is entitled for 300 units. Combined, they only add about 1,100 units to the housing stock.

Four

A couple of smaller buildings are already selling, including the 98-unit Marlow (Van Ness and Clay) and the 63-unit 300 Ivy (at Gough). Both have strong buyer interest, and both are releasing units in stages and escalating prices as they do. Next up will be 21-unit 2000 Ellis at Divisadero and 115-unit Linea at 1998 Market. The total is a mere 300 more units, and some of them are BMRs.

Five

At the end of April 2013, San Francisco's unemployment rate was 5.4 percent, down from a peak of 9.9 percent in February 2010. Moretti's book sheds light on why this is so.

Bubble, Smubble!
September 2013

Clients and colleagues are asking me whether San Francisco's residential prices will keep increasing or whether we're in a bubble that will soon burst. Prices averaged more than 10 percent appreciation in 2012 over 2011, and this year we're up some 20 percent over 2012 through July. In my opinion, while these double-digit rates are not sustainable, we are not in a bubble.

There are key drivers that will keep residential real estate appreciating.

Back from the Burbs

In 1956, President Eisenhower signed into law the Interstate Highway Act, which was the catalyst for many families to leave the urban core and move to the suburbs. Several recent studies say that the trend has reversed.

Single-family homeowners with a front lawn, a two-car garage, a backyard for BBQs, and a quiet street where kids can play are now burdened with long commute times, higher energy costs, and a lack of connectedness. Urban cores allow for walking/biking to work, lower gasoline bills, more diversity, and more chances to connect and interact with others.

In the forty years from 1930 to 1970, San Francisco's population grew only 12.8 percent, or from 634,394 to 715,674. The entire Bay Area almost tripled from 1,578,009 in 1930 to 4,630,576 in 1970, and today its population is 7.4 million.

Today San Francisco has a population a touch over 800,000. The forecast, however, is for it to grow to 900,000 or more by 2030! Where are all those people going to live? For a good perspective on the move from the suburbs to the city, I suggest that you read *The New Geography of Jobs*.

Venture Capital

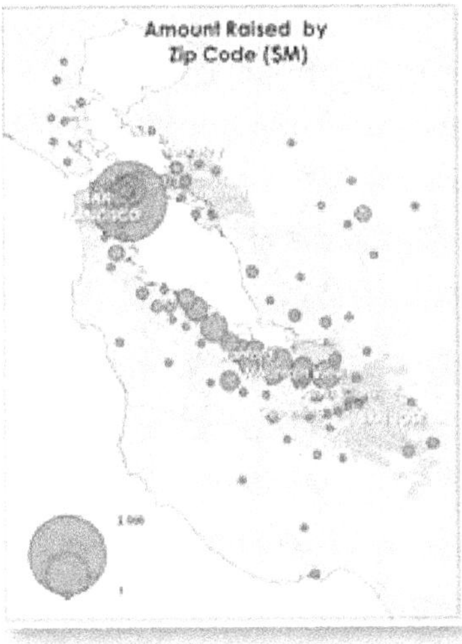

According to Richard Florida, author of *Who's Your City?*, San Francisco may be the new Silicon Valley. In the 1980s, 1990s and 2000s, not a single urban center rivaled Silicon Valley as the center of high-tech start-ups.

In 2011, the city of San Francisco was the leading venture-capital investment center, garnering $4.39 billion, roughly a third of that of the Bay Area, and a whopping 16 percent of the total venture-capital investment nationally. Palo Alto was a distant second with $1.29 billion, and Redwood City garnered $1.09 billion. Silicon Valley, San Francisco, Oakland, and the surrounding areas attracted $13.5 billion in venture capital, an amount four times more than that of the greater Boston area or the greater New York area.

The City Is the Place to Be

- Though he founded PayPal in a coffee shop on University Avenue in Palo Alto, Paul Thiel has established his venture fund in San Francisco rather than in Silicon Valley.
- While Yahoo and Facebook have their corporate campuses in Sunnyvale and Menlo Park, respectively, their CEOs have chosen to live in homes in the city.
- The city has become an attractor of start-ups that then attract jobs, which attract more talent.
- Who wants to drive two miles to get a quart of milk?

While the recent pace of residential appreciation may abate some, San Francisco's ability to gestate new companies that create more tech jobs along with commensurate wealth augurs well for residential demand to continue with robust appreciation. There is no land on which to build single-family homes, and it takes the patience of Job and major funding to weather the procedural processes to build new apartments and condominiums. Those who are unable to buy will rent. Those who can buy will compete and raise prices.

My Top-Ten List
May 2014

The Price of Progress

If you asked me to list the top-ten topics about San Francisco real estate that capture my attention, the list would be the following:

- gentrification
- Google buses
- overcrowding
- skyrocketing rental prices
- the Twitter tax break
- congestion
- population explosion
- cranes in the sky
- impacted views
- first responders at risk

Years ago, the principal San Francisco industries were banking, insurance, legal, advertising, and real estate. High tech was booming, although it was centered in Silicon Valley with companies like HP, Cisco, Intuit, Apple, Microsoft, Google, eBay, Oracle, Genentech, and others, along with a community of venture capitalists.

As these Valley power players matured, they opened San Francisco offices. Then came the likes of Salesforce, Twitter, Zynga, Square, Yelp, Airbnb, Dropbox, Adobe, and Dolby.

While Facebook, Samsung, Google, and Apple are in the process of building huge Valley campuses, many employees prefer to live in the city, where they can hop on a bus to the Valley campus. A few companies—like Salesforce, LinkedIn, and Splunk, all of which are located south of Market Street—are creating vertical campuses in downtown San Francisco.

We all know that tech money is driving a lot of our residential fervor. The downtown activity is also driving prices to new heights in those neighborhoods within walking (or biking) distance to jobs, most notably Hayes Valley, Inner Mission, Potrero Hill, and Bernal Heights. While the overall residential market is hot, these neighborhoods are hot, hot!

Gosh, San Francisco Is So Expensive September 2014

I keep hearing this. Is it?

Certainly, when you compare us to Dallas, Philadelphia, Houston, or Detroit, the answer is yes. When you compare us to Hong Kong, New York, Singapore, Moscow, and other "great" cities, I'm not so sure.

The natives are mostly commenting on the cost of living, and the biggest cost-of-living item is real estate. Whether you're renting or buying, San Francisco is indeed expensive.

Kids are a major culprit. Besides needing to be fed and clothed, they take up room, and for some reason, they need to be educated—for a very long time. At $25,000 or more per year per kid in private school, it gets to be expensive—and we are talking about after tax dollars. Alternatively, we have public schools, but when I talk to parents about SF public schools, I'm told that those in East Bay, Marin, and the Peninsula are usually the best.

Planning Ahead Pied-à-Terre/Empty Nester February 2015

Pied-à-Terre

San Francisco has always offered opportunities to enjoy dining, entertainment, sightseeing, and other activities that don't exist as much in Modesto, Sacramento, Roseville, or Los Gatos.

After a while, the family conversation may lead to a question: "Why don't we consider buying a place in the city?" When that conversation does occur, a few key things should be considered.

Start small. Buying a pied-à-terre can be a good test for the next stage—that is, being an empty nester and relocating one's primary residence to the city. By starting small, you limit your financial commitment, and you can "test" whether you actually want to live in the city part time or full time without making an all-out commitment.

Empty Nester

The next stage is packing up the old homestead, where the children were raised, BBQs were enjoyed, and neighbors stopped by on occasion. Taking care of a single-family home may get to be a hassle over time, and some bedrooms may remain vacant much of the time. Perhaps it is time to move to the city.

Simplifying one's life becomes important. That means reducing the need to maintain a home and backyard; worrying less about property security when traveling; and being able to enjoy dining, entertainment, and shopping without making fifty-mile round trips. Our automobiles are depreciating assets, notwithstanding lower prices at the pump, and the city now has extensive car sharing and on-call car networks.

Assuming that you've tested city living with a pied-à-terre, the decision of where to put down new roots becomes less difficult. The experience of owning a pied-à-terre facilitates the decision-making process concerning whether to buy a more permanent home—that is, one for the rest of your life.

GO WEST, YOUNG MAN/WOMAN
AUGUST 2015

Two articles caught my eye this month: one was about the Obama administration's alums beating a path to San Francisco start-ups, and one was about Wall Street executives doing the same. Both are affecting the upper end of the San Francisco residential market—both rentals and for-sale homes.

Why?

Technology was a central component of Obama's presidential campaign, so tech companies are a logical next step for many. "If you're writing for a CEO out here, they're more likely to be your peer than your grandfather," says Tommy Vietor, a former National Security Council spokesman who has a speech-writing consulting firm in San Francisco. "They're young, they're cool, and they get it."

The *San Francisco Business Journal* reports that recent arrivals at Uber include David Plouffe, who ran President Obama's 2008 campaign; Jessica Santillo, a former White House assistant press secretary; Jordan Burke, the former White House director of strategic and message initiatives; Kellyn Blossom, associate director of intergovernmental affairs; and Sarah Fenn, an assistant to the deputy White House chief of staff.

Salesforce recruited Jim Green, Obama's campaign staff director for technology, and Obama's former CIO, Vivek Kundra. Twitter snagged Katie Jacobs Stanton, the administration's director of citizen participation, while Airbnb hired Obama administration alums Nick Papas, John Baldo, Courtney O'Donnell, and Clark Stevens. Square hired Michelle Obama's former deputy communications director, Semonti Stephens, and Nest brought in Obama's former speechwriter Kyle O'Connor.

From Wall Street, recent additions to San Francisco include Ruth Porat from Morgan Stanley, who became Google's CFO; Sarah Friar, a Goldman alum who is now CFO of Square; and ex–Goldman banker Anthony Noto, who is now Twitter's CFO.

So?

These are not your computer-science geeks. They are highly paid nontechie executives able to pay $10,000 or more per month for a rental and $5 million or more for a purchase. They are competing with the nontech world of relocating executives, empty nesters, newly minted millionaires with IPO cash, foreign buyers looking for a safe haven, investors, and others with a lot of money.

The year 2015 was the fourth straight year with 10 or more percent average annual appreciation. These new arrivals are another addition to the buyer mix that supports this heady market and raises average prices.

Wait and See
September 2015

"Wait and see" is neither a plan nor a strategy. I'm talking about waiting to buy into our hot condominium market. Potential buyers are easily discouraged after being beaten by competition time after time. The competition is intense, and prices are through the roof; "I'll wait and see" is the equivalent of throwing in the towel.

Client Story

Back in the dark ages—that would be 2004—a client decided to buy a condominium and to forgo renting. She set her sights on a condominium in Cow Hollow. It needed work, like a new kitchen, a new bath, and new wiring, not to mention painting and other cosmetic work. It was listed for $699,000, and there were ten offers. She won the property with an offer of $801,000, 14.5 percent over the list price. Crazy?

My economics/financial education made me question the rationality of bidding so high. We looked at the average price appreciation of San Francisco condominiums for the previous twenty years. It was about 7 percent per year. So I said to my client, "Client, let's say the property is really 'worth' six hundred ninety-nine thousand dollars. At what point in the future could you be made 'whole' [i.e., sell it for the price paid] if the market appreciates only five percent per year?" The answer? It would take only three years, and since she was planning to remain in San Francisco for at least five or more years, it was a no-brainer.

The Market

The average price of condominiums citywide during the three-year period 2001–2003 was *down 6.7 percent.* Average prices were up about 16 percent per year in both 2004 and 2005. Then the economy tanked in 2008, and prices dived 16 percent between 2009 and 2011. Prices rebounded more than 10 percent a year in 2012, 2013, and 2014, and prices are up 14 percent so far in 2015.

The long-term trend is up, and there will be periodical downturns because life and real estate are cyclical!

Inventory and Supply

Here are my rough estimates of San Francisco housing stock:

Apartment units	300,000—66 percent
Single-family homes	110,000
Condominiums	45,000
Total housing stock	455,000

In other words, two thirds of the housing stock consists of rentals. Condominium resales (not new construction) will account for about 2,600 units in 2015, or about 5.8 percent of the overall condominium stock (which implies that owners move, on average, every seventeen or so years).

In the meantime, we see all sorts of cranes throughout the city. Some are for office buildings, some are for hospitals, and some are for apartment or condominium buildings. While there are many condominium buildings under construction, most have fewer than one hundred units, and fewer than nine hundred new units in the city will be delivered in 2015. This hardly makes a dent in the housing stock.

Illustration by Duane Bryers

The bottom line is that we can't build fast enough. There are many reasons. What really matters is that "wait and see" doesn't get you into a property. I suggest that you hold your nose and jump in as long as you plan to own for five or more years. There's one caveat: you'd best have a (really) good agent when you buy to ensure a successful exit when you sell.

Are We Getting Tired?
December 2015

I've started to see a number of price reductions—more than in previous months—and the chatter among my fellow agents is that the market is weakening. A recent article about Square's IPO and the valuation of other unicorns got me thinking.

Is the Market Getting Tired?

We've been in an up cycle since 2011. This is the fourth year of robust appreciation (better than 10 percent a year). The up cycle from 1994 to 2000 lasted for seven years and ended with the dot-com bust. The next up leg was 2004 to 2008, and it ended with the great recession (which caused an economic downturn of about three years). We are probably closer to the end of this up cycle than to the beginning, but no one knows how close we are.

While the current up leg may be getting a bit long in the tooth, my crystal ball says that it is not headed south; there will probably be slower growth in the year ahead rather than a continuation of the double-digit growth that we've seen for these last four years.

Psychology

Even though our residential real estate benefits from multiple buyer groups (five legs to the stool) that sustain a vibrant market over the long term, changing market psychology also plays a role in and contributes to mini-cycles within the long-term upward trend.

Square had its IPO on November 19 at an offer price of nine dollars a share, a decrease of 50 percent from its most recent private financing a year ago. I've read that major mutual funds—ones that have been investors in start-ups over the past decade—have started to mark down the valuations of some of their private-company holdings.

Here's a question: Is the bloom off of high-tech stocks? Is this contributing to changing (short-term) real estate psychology? My monthly numbers don't indicate any drop-off in appreciation. (We are up some 13.5 percent over last year through the end of November.) Given where we are in the cycle, it would seem that the heady 10 percent or more per year appreciation rate is coming to an end, though I know not when.

But as I have said many times, it doesn't matter, since it's the long game that makes San Francisco residential real estate attractive.

CHAPTER 2

Newer Neighborhoods

The opening of AT&T Park in March 2000 was the catalyst for the dramatic construction that has taken place in the last fifteen years, first in south of Market (SOMA), then in South Beach, then in Yerba Buena, and then in Mission Bay.

Just as AT&T Park sparked construction developments in adjacent neighborhoods, there are more than a half dozen other major developments that will impact a number of other San Francisco neighborhoods.

There are at least five major developments taking shape. They include the Transbay Terminal and 5 M (Fifth and Mission Street) downtown, Warriors Arena and Sea Wall Lot 337 in Mission Bay, and Pier 70 in Dogpatch.

Then there are the Shipyard in Bayview at the southern end of the city and Treasure Island in the middle of the bay, both of which are massive developments with a planned capacity of more than eight thousand residential units.

SOUTH OF MARKET STREET AUGUST 2005

Over the past six months, I have had a number of conversations with clients about selling their homes in one of the more established neighborhoods of San Francisco and moving into a "full-service" building in a neighborhood south of Market Street.

The area south of Market Street is undergoing dramatic change. Even if you don't have an interest in this area of the city, it's wise to understand the change afoot, since it will likely impact the value of residential real estate throughout the city. Here's why: Say you're selling your condominium in the Marina, Cow Hollow, or Russian Hill. Some of your potential buyers may opt to buy south of Market, thus reducing the demand for your home.

Rincon Hill

The San Francisco Planning Commission adopted a new plan for Rincon Hill in May 2005. It encompasses approximately fifty-five acres subdivided into more than seventy parcels. You can see the outlines of the Rincon Hill area in the accompanying map.

Transbay Redevelopment District

San Francisco is blessed with an abundance of high-quality open spaces, including large parks like Golden Gate Park and the

Presidio and smaller parks like Alamo Square, Lafayette, and the Alta Vista Parks. It has walking neighborhoods such as Polk Street, Union Street, Chestnut Street, Twenty-Fourth Street, and many others.

The Transbay Terminal and its surrounding areas are another story. Their streets are configured to carry traffic efficiently without providing pedestrian amenities. The entire area is a gritty, noisy, polluted environment devoted almost entirely to the movement of cars, trucks, and transit vehicles. This is in the process of changing, and although the transformation will not be completed until 2015 or later, prospective buyers would be wise to understand what is planned.

Folsom Boulevard

Folsom Boulevard is intended to be a seam that will join the Transbay and Rincon Hill neighborhoods. The plan is for an amenity-rich, tree-enhanced boulevard that will be lined with retail, restaurant, and community space with wider-than-normal sidewalks and a generous number of trees and other streetscape amenities for pedestrians. Think of an enhanced Chestnut and/or Polk Street with better traffic circulation and parking and an overall better ambiance (that's the plan, anyway). If this plan does take shape as envisioned, Folsom Boulevard could become an important location consideration.

Mission Bay

Mission Bay is an area south of Rincon Hill. It includes the ballpark and stretches south to Mariposa Street, and it's bordered on the west by the 280 Freeway. It includes existing and new developments along King Street and Berry Street, and to the south it will include over five million square feet for office, laboratory, research, manufacturing, and multimedia uses.

I suggest that if you haven't already done so, take a drive through the area that is about to become a major new center of biotech and life sciences.

A Supply-Demand Perspective

According to the San Francisco Planning Department, there were a total of 354,063 housing units in the city at the end of 2004, approximately 65 percent of which were in the rental pool, which means that roughly 124,000 properties were owner occupied. My best estimate is that there are 85,000 single-family homes and that the 39,000 other properties are the owner units in buildings with 2 to 10 or more units.

In the entire city, 8,389 new units were constructed, including new rental and affordable-housing units, during the four-year period from 2001 to 2004; on average, there were about 2,100 new units each year.

Some 15,000 or more condominium units are being constructed or approved or are in the planning/conception stage. Even if all 15,000 units are built, which is probably not going to happen, they will not come to market at the same time; most likely, they will come to market over a ten-year period. I end up with an *average annual addition to inventory of 1,500 units.*

Looking Out to 2015

The big draws to date for the south of Market area have been AT&T Park, good weather, the fact that it's walking distance from the Financial District, moderate prices, and some good views.

A number of the new towers are going to be architecturally interesting and tall. The towers at 300 Spear and 201 Folsom will be about thirty-five and forty stories, respectively. The building at 301 Mission will be fifty-eight stories, and One Rincon Hill at 425 First Street will have two towers, one with forty-nine stories and one with sixty-one stories.

The First Street Corridor

The Metropolitan with 298 units at 333–355 First Street sold out quickly earlier this year. If you want to be close to the Bay Bridge on-ramp, this is a great location, but other than that, I don't quite get it. First Street is the main feeder route to the Bay Bridge, and from four to six in the evening on any given workday, it is pretty clogged. In addition, some of the existing views will be diminished by planned new towers.

Summary

The key point I'm sharing is that purchasing a property in the south of Market Street area, whether it be in Rincon Hill, Mission Bay, or the Transbay area, is more complicated than buying a home in an established area like the Richmond, Noe Valley, or Marina. One needs to consider not only the location and amenities of the new project being offered but also the projects that may be offered over the next several years and the amenities that will be put in place (and where they'll be put) by the city and developers. What might have been the best location in 2005 may not be the best on a competitive basis in five or ten years. Also, what is taking place south of Market Street will have an economic impact on residential real estate values throughout the city.

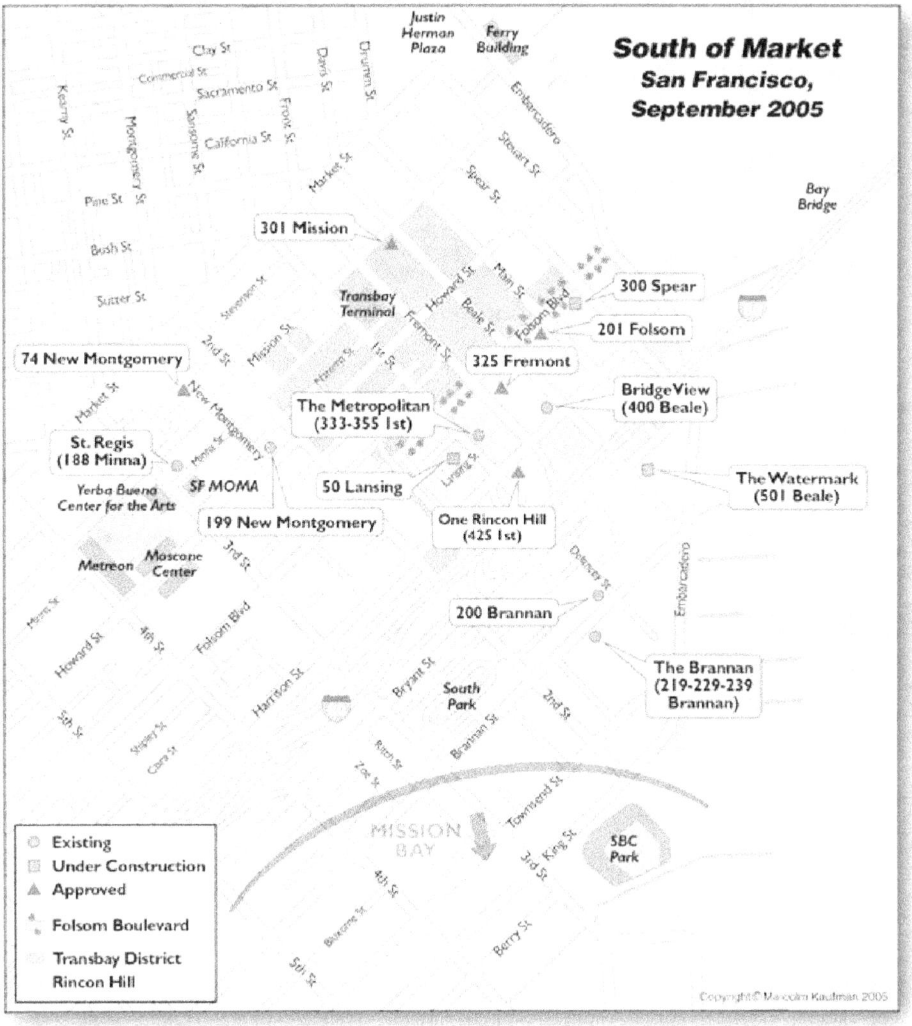
South of Market
San Francisco,
September 2005
Justin Herman Plaza
Ferry Building
Clay St
Commercial St
Sacramento St
California St
Kearny St
Montgomery St
Sansome St
Front St
Davis St
Drumm St
Embarcadero
Steuart St
Spear St
Market St
Pine St
Bush St
Sutter St
Bay Bridge
301 Mission
Transbay Terminal
Howard St
Main St
Beale St
Folsom Blvd
300 Spear
201 Folsom
Stevenson St
2nd St
Mission St
Fremont St
1st St
74 New Montgomery
325 Fremont
BridgeView
(400 Beale)
New Montgomery
The Metropolitan
(333-355 1st)
St. Regis
(188 Minna)
50 Lansing
Lansing St
The Watermark
(501 Beale)
Yerba Buena
Center for the Arts
SF MOMA
199 New Montgomery
One Rincon Hill
(425 1st)
3rd St
Metreon
Moscone Center
Delancey St
200 Brannan
Howard St
4th St
Folsom Blvd
The Brannan
(219-229-239
Brannan)
Harrison St
Bryant St
South Park
2nd St
5th St
Brannan St
Townsend St
MISSION BAY
King St
3rd St
SBC Park
4th St
Berry St
5th St
Existing
Under Construction
Approved
Folsom Boulevard
Transbay District
Rincon Hill
Copyright© Malcolm Kaufman 2005

A view of downtown San Francisco from Treasure Island

A rendering of the future San Francisco landscape

Images by Peter Bosselmann/Urban Explorer, courtesy of the San Francisco Planning Department

Mission Bay
March 2007

Recent History

I guess that the first time I visited South Mission Bay was about three years ago, when I decided to try the golf driving range to enhance my golf swing (to no avail). The next time I was there was for a tour of the Gladstone Institute and the Genentech Hall, where I watched a researcher inject a rat with an esoteric chemical in an effort to gain a better understanding of Parkinson's disease. I am sure that the rat made the ultimate sacrifice.

The area has changed dramatically just in the last few years! It's mind-boggling, what's going on.

Redevelopment

Most of the real estate talk in San Francisco is usually about square feet. In Mission Bay we're talking about acreage—some 303 acres of land between the San Francisco Bay and Interstate 280.

The first image at the end of this *Pulse* is an aerial-view taken about a year ago. Take a look: it won't be long before this image becomes a historical artifact. The driving range is still seen to the left of the center of the image, just to the right of Interstate 280, and the Old Navy building is to the right of the center. In the center foreground is a cluster of bio-tech and life-sciences facilities that represent the start of a very ambitious program to make Mission

Bay as important to the life-science community as Silicon Valley is to the semiconductor/computer industry.

Development will take place over the next ten to fifteen years and will include the following:

- six thousand housing units
- six million square feet of office/life-science/technology commercial space,
- a new UCSF research campus containing 2.65 million square feet of building space on forty-three acres
- five hundred thousand square feet of retail space
- a five-hundred-room hotel
- forty or more acres of public open space, including parks along Mission Creek and the bay
- a new five-hundred-student public school, a new public library, and new fire and police stations

The Start of Residential

My interest in Mission Bay was piqued by Noe Valley clients who wanted warmer weather and a simplified lifestyle, including updated construction and amenities—a story that is becoming more familiar to me each year.

We have been talking on and off for a year about their moving to one of the buildings south of Mission Creek. The area is unfolding as less urban than the developments of South Beach, Rincon Hill, and Transbay and remains quite close to the Financial District. It has lookouts to the bay and is in easy walking distance to my favorite funky Ramp restaurant. A drawback is its current lack of neighborhood amenities. It will take a while for the planned Fourth Street to become the Chestnut Street of Mission Bay. The light-rail is now running on Third Street and will connect to the downtown area.

The entire area is now under construction. It's totally different than any other San Francisco neighborhood. The juxtaposition of research, commercial, and retail facilities; residential areas; and some of the best weather in San Francisco is an interesting feature not found elsewhere in the city.

Mission Bay, circa 2007

SOMA Update June 2007

Back in September 2005, I took a stab at reviewing the major developments south of Market Street (SOMA). It was my first attempt to convey the magnitude to which the South Beach, Rincon Hill, Transbay, and Mission Bay neighborhoods are being transformed. Since that time I've devoted many hours of research to learning about this area. Despite the fact that I'm better informed today, two years later, I continue to feel overwhelmed by the number and diversity of existing developments, not to mention those under construction and on the planning boards. I see no letup in south of Market developments.

Lots of Choices

Look at the map. The map includes only major buildings; smaller buildings are not shown. Buyers are facing even more opportunities than the map depicts.

It is particularly daunting for a buyer who lives in Silicon Valley or North or East Bay and wants a place in San Francisco. How does one make sense of all this?

Timing

There are fourteen buildings shown completed and ready to be moved in to. This is great for those who want a home now. They can buy and close soon and actually inspect the unit to see what they're getting.

For other buyers, a yet-to-be-completed building may be attractive because it may fit a need for a delayed close, whether that close will take place in three or eighteen months. These folks can keep an eye on the future as the development landscape unfolds.

Summing Up

One thing a buyer can't do, in my opinion, is time the market. Some people tell me that they're sitting on the sidelines, waiting for supply to overpower demand and to drive prices down. I don't think you can time the stock market, and I don't think it makes sense to attempt to time the San Francisco residential market. What is clear is that average *annual* condominium prices have appreciated over the last twenty years at 7or more percent, and developer construction costs are not likely to go down.

The scope and pace of development in SOMA is exciting and overwhelming. Having a good guide, whether you choose me or someone else, is essential to making an educated decision in the midst of so many opportunities. Making a wrong decision can be costly. Paying several hundred thousand dollars for a view today only to have it obstructed in a few years is not a smart investment decision. Such an error can be avoided, or certainly mitigated, with research and knowledge.

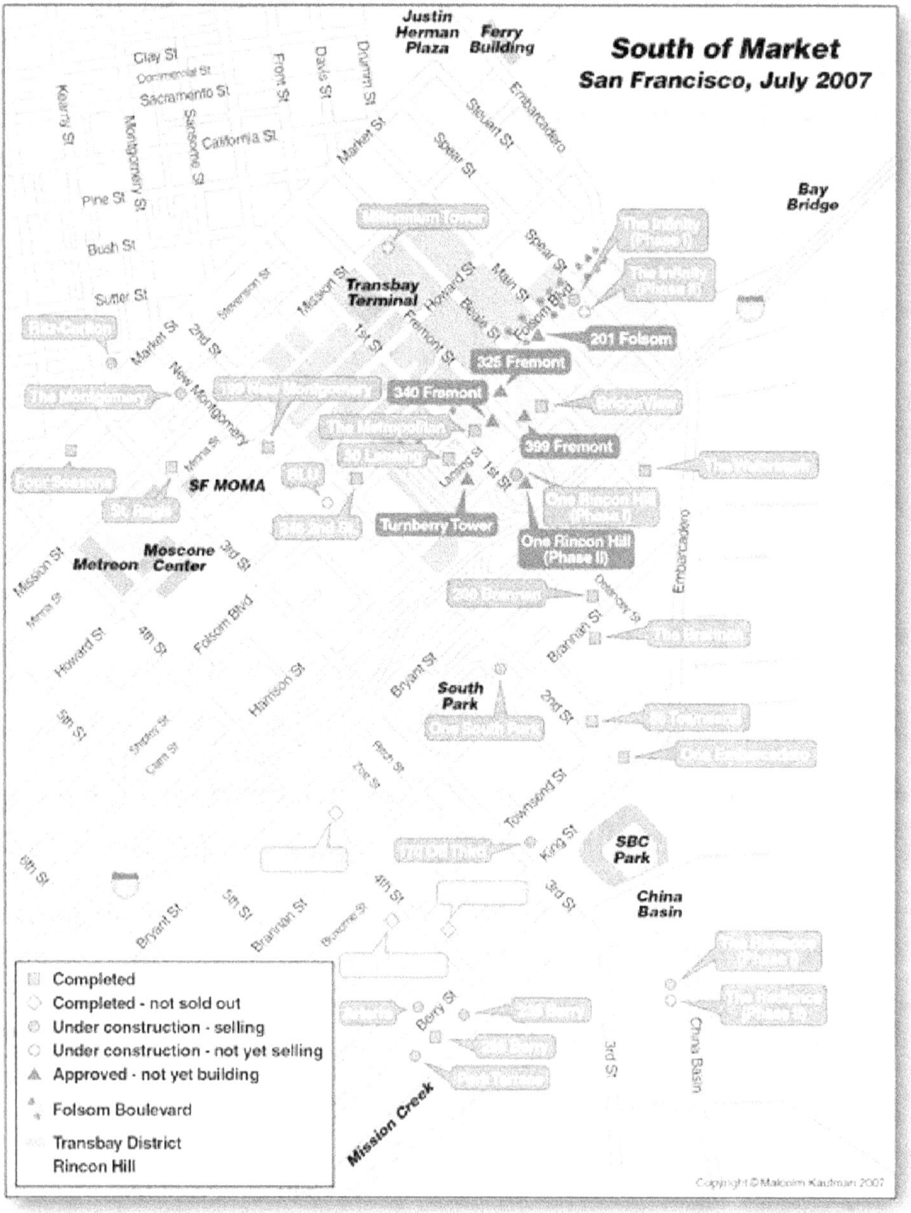
South of Market
San Francisco, July 2007
Justin Herman Plaza
Ferry Building
Bay Bridge
Clay St
Sacramento St
California St
Pine St
Bush St
Sutter St
Kearny St
Montgomery St
Sansome St
Front St
Davis St
Drumm St
Market St
Steuart St
Spear St
Embarcadero
Transbay Terminal
Mission St
Howard St
Main St
Beale St
Fremont St
Folsom Blvd
1st St
2nd St
New Montgomery
201 Folsom
325 Fremont
340 Fremont
399 Fremont
Turnberry Tower
One Rincon Hill (Phase II)
SF MOMA
Moscone Center
Metreon
3rd St
4th St
5th St
6th St
Folsom Blvd
Harrison St
Bryant St
Brannan St
South Park
Townsend St
King St
SBC Park
China Basin
Berry St
Mission Creek
Completed
Completed - not sold out
Under construction - selling
Under construction - not yet selling
Approved - not yet building
Folsom Boulevard
Transbay District
Rincon Hill
Copyright © Malcolm Kaufman 2007

Transbay
September 2007

In November 2006, I devoted a *Pulse* to the new Westfield Centre at Fifth and Mission, discussing its impact on the downtown area. To quote myself (wow, is that egotistical!), "According to Mayor Gavin Newsom, this new center expects twenty-five million visitors a year and $600 million in annual mall revenues. Bloomingdales and Westfield are influencing the future and, in the process, are changing the world. They are transforming the midmarket corridor of San Francisco. They are betting a lot of money, and they are smart people, not gamblers."

By all accounts, the center has been very successful since its opening almost a year ago.

The Transbay Transit Center

Like the Westfield Centre, the Transbay Center (see the street-location map) will have a major positive impact on the greater south of Market Street area and probably on the entire city.

The goal is to create "the Grand Central Station of the West," replacing the Transbay terminal now located at First Street and Mission Street.

Part of the dream is to build a California high-speed rail system that will connect San Francisco with Sacramento to the north and with Los Angeles and San Diego to the south. The plan also includes extending Caltrain 1.3 miles underground from its current terminus at Fourth Street and Townsend Street to the proposed transit center.

The map depicts the transit center at the top and the underground extension to the Caltrain Station at the bottom.

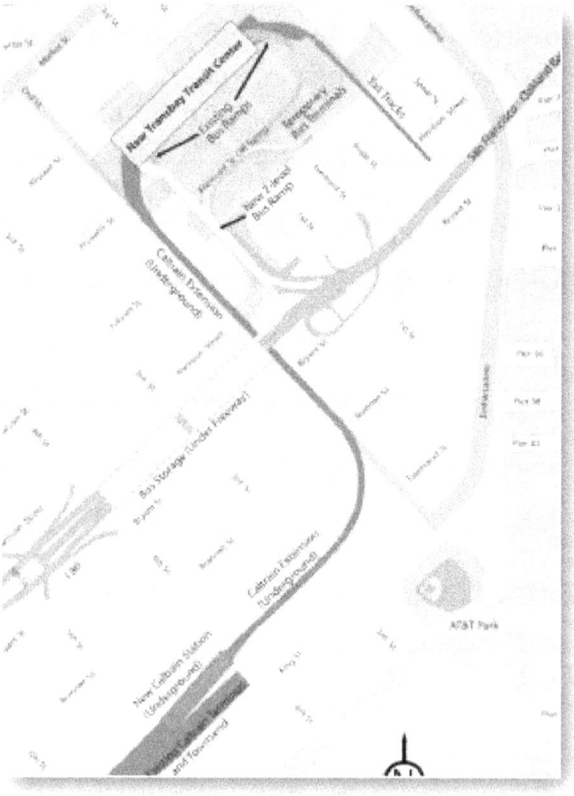

Construction is tentatively scheduled to begin in 2009. In addition to the transit center, there will be a twelve-hundred-foot (eighty-floor) glass-wrapped tower adjacent to the terminal. The plan is for the tower to include 1.6 million square feet of commercial office space; it will likely be some of the most expensive commercial space in the city. One of the attributes of the plan is a 5.4-acre elevated park on top of the terminal complex.

It's Still Early

I think the Transbay Transit Center and Tower will have an enormously positive impact on residential real estate throughout the city of San Francisco—and not just on a few neighborhoods south of Market Street. Think of the millions of people who will be able to visit the city with much more ease—not only those from the surrounding Bay Area communities but, if the high-speed rail system gets built, also folks who live in Sacramento, Los Angeles, and San Diego. They'll be able to hop on a train and be here in between two and four hours—and bypass airport hassles.

The *Chronicle* ran an article a few days ago featuring the soon-to-open Barneys just off of Union Square. The article said that "considering how small San Francisco is, we are second strongest for the retail market in the country, meaning second only to New York in gross sales."

That's one big statement, and if true, it's further justification that the business and residential outlook for San Francisco is quite rosy.

The easier it is for people to get here and to enjoy pleasant surroundings, the more they'll want to come and spend on consumer goods, dining, entertainment, and residences. I think the Transbay Center and Tower are buffo, in case you couldn't tell.

TRANSBAY UPDATE
JANUARY 2010

More than two years ago, in September 2007, I first wrote about the planned Transbay Transit Center expected to reshape a whole swath of real estate around Mission Street and First Street.

This is one huge, breathtaking undertaking. It's such an exciting, impactful project that I thought an update would be worthwhile.

Transbay Joint Powers Authority

The Schedule

Construction of the new Transbay Transit Center will take about five years and is expected to be completed after 2015.

The schedule gets a bit fuzzier concerning the California high-speed rail line that would terminate at the Transit Center and connect Southern California with San Francisco and other Northern California communities. Also, there does not seem to be a timetable for the construction of the 1,200-foot tower that would serve as one of the focal points of the transit center. The tower is expected to house commercial rather than residential space.

Dreaming

The new Transbay Transit Center will assemble under one roof the nine modes of transportation that presently serve the Bay Area. It is intended to make it easy for people to switch between various modes of transportation. The "city-park" that will sit above the facility will serve as an attractive, generous amenity for the up-and-coming south of Market Street neighborhoods. It will also double as a green roof for the transit facility.

Once completed, the new transit center is expected to serve forty-five million passengers a year, eliminate eight thousand automobile trips daily, and tie Silicon Valley and other parts of the Bay Area to San Francisco more neatly.

The plan to extend the Caltrain commuter line (underground) from the current Townsend and Fourth Street station to the new transit center is a huge undertaking in itself and is not expected to start until sometime after 2014.

I suspect that the transit center, when completed, will become a world-recognized San Francisco architectural jewel and contribute economically to the city.

Can you image hopping on a train and spending the weekend in Los Angeles after a two-and-a-half-hour ride? Or more importantly, can you imagine the economic benefits to our economy, residential real estate, and other segments of San Francisco when the eighteen million people who live in the Los Angeles metro area can shop, eat, and own property only two and a half hours to the north? Bring it on!

The Optimist
July 2010

There are two anchors being dropped at the north and south ends of the area south of Market Street. In due course, they will have a positive impact on adjoining residential real estate. One is the Transbay Terminal at Mission at First Street and Fremont Street, and the other is Seawall Lot 337 in Mission Bay just south of AT&T Park. Two other improvements will also be positives: the expansion of the SF MOMA to accommodate the Fisher modern-art collection and Forest City's work to improve the area around the Metreon. Take a look at the map to get your bearings.

North/South Anchors

Demolition of the existing bus terminal is scheduled to start in August. In its place will rise the Transbay Terminal, a.k.a. "the Grand Central Station of the West." Just south of AT&T Park in Mission Bay is a multifaceted development that is gaining traction under the auspices of the port authority.

It goes by the titillating name of Seawall Lot 337. The land, much of which is currently used for parking, will be used for new offices, housing, shopping, entertainment, and open space. It will bring new vibrancy to Mission Bay, which continues to grow as the country's life-sciences hub. The Radiance will benefit as well.

In the Middle

Both the Metreon and the SF MOMA, at the western and eastern ends of Moscone Center, are undergoing their own changes. The SF MOMA is planning a new southern facade, one that will house the Fisher modern-art collection bequeathed to the museum last year. While plans need to be drawn and money, raised, the direction, if not the timetable, is clear: the SF MOMA will be the home to one of the most unique art collections in the world, which will be yet another reason for people to live and visit south of Market Street.

The Antagonists

On June 25, 2010, the *San Francisco Business Times* published an article called "Supes might make high-rises endangered species." The article notes that there are more habitats for butterflies than high-rises on Rincon Hill these days, and a growing number of San Francisco slow-growth advocates like it that way.

It is already difficult to obtain financing for new condominium developments, and the board of supervisors makes it exceedingly difficult for a developer to launch a new project. Three pieces of land on Freemont Street (numbers 325, 340, and 399) are sprouting flowers/butterflies. However, there are no flowers or butterflies at 201 Folsom, the future home of the second Infinity complex. Meanwhile, some people in the city actually think that we should have more housing!

The Optimist

Notwithstanding the killer-bee instincts of the board of supervisors, the port authority, the SF MOMA, and Forest City are making south of Market Street a better place to work, live, and visit. Before long, construction lenders will lend, developers will develop, supervisors will bend, and new homes will be built.

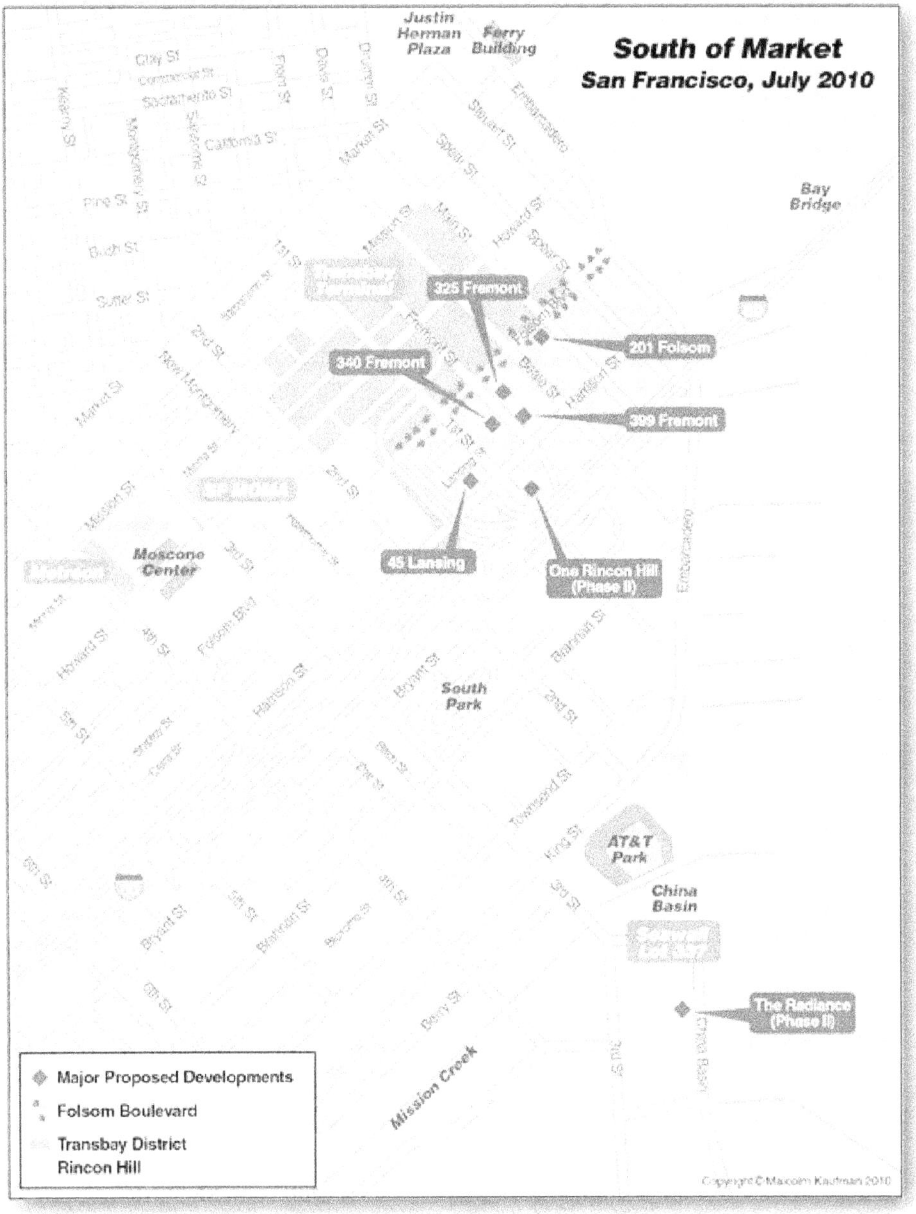
South of Market
San Francisco, July 2010
Justin Herman Plaza
Ferry Building
Bay Bridge
325 Fremont
201 Folsom
340 Fremont
399 Fremont
45 Lansing
One Rincon Hill (Phase II)
Moscone Center
South Park
AT&T Park
China Basin
The Radiance (Phase II)
Mission Creek
Major Proposed Developments
Folsom Boulevard
Transbay District
Rincon Hill
Copyright © Malcolm Kaufman 2010

Commercial/Residential Symbiosis May 2011

According to the media, south of Market Street commercial space is hot, while that of the traditional Financial District is not. Commercial brokers put it this way: tech demand is outstripping traditional core demand (e.g., demand for lawyers, bankers, and insurers). Tech is hiring; traditional is not. Ergo, leasing rates are rising south of Market Street because that's where the tech folks want to be. Brick and timber are cool—glass and steel, not so much.

The condominium buildings south of Market Street contain some ten thousand units, or about 25 percent of San Francisco's condominium housing stock; 90 percent of those units did not exist fifteen years ago. From a residential point of view, south of Market is cool, and in some cases, like commercial, it commands higher prices than condominiums on the north end of town—namely in Pacific Heights, Presidio Heights, Cow Hollow, Russian Hill, and Nob Hill. In the last six months, the sale of south of Market condos of $1.2 million or more outpaced sales in the more traditional neighborhoods by a margin of two to one.

By and large, the bay views north of Market are much better than they are in South Beach, Yerba Buena, or SOMA. Views are very important, but they're not everything. There are other issues at play here, including cool architecture and who your business neighbors are. Many upper-end residential buyers prefer a top-notch amenity package and the benefits of modern construction more than the kind of architecturally attractive 1920s building that can be found north of Market Street but not south of it.

What was important ten or more years ago may be less important today for both segments of the market.

Trends change, often when there's a catalyst for change. AT&T Park opened in March 2000 and was a major catalyst for the residential development south of Market Street. In Mission Bay, Genentech Hall was the first building at the UCSF Research Campus. It was the spark for biotech and life-science companies and encouraged Bosa Development to pioneer residential construction. There's no doubt that Twitter's planned move to Tenth and Market will act as a catalyst to midmarket neighborhood development. And the beat goes on.

Each morning numerous Bauer buses troll the streets of San Francisco for employees who commute to the traditional locations of the tech community, like Palo Alto, Santa Clara, and Sunnyvale. At the same time, many of these same tech companies have leased major space in the city because many of their employees prefer to live and work in the city. The city is vibrant, diverse, and cool. It's a fun place to be.

The eighty or more new residential buildings south of Market Street have changed the landscape. They have added permanent residents who remain in the area after five in evening. They are there on the weekends, and they have brought restaurants and retail, which in turn bring more high-tech commercial spaces.

MISSION BAY: GREAT OPPORTUNITY, TRICKY MARKET JULY 2011

With the March 2000 opening of AT&T Park serving as a catalyst to growth, the neighborhoods South Beach, Yerba Buena, SOMA, and Mission Bay (north of Mission Creek) started taking off. Notwithstanding the economic downturn, these neighborhoods have blossomed commercially and residentially. Now there is significant action south of Mission Creek.

What Are We Talking About?

Mission Bay's Major Properties

Mission Bay was an unattractive rail yard owned by the Southern Pacific Railroad Company. In 1998, Mayor Willie Brown got UCSF involved, then the Giants opened AT&T Park in 2000, and then Vancouver-based Bosa Development snapped up most of the land zoned for market-rate residential and built the ninety-nine-unit Radiance. Salesforce.com made a deal for fourteen acres toward the end of 2010.

What Makes It Special?

Mission Bay is not a typical San Francisco neighborhood. First of all, it's brand new. It was just a lot of dirt until recently, and it's not yet "finished." The rest of the city is pretty much "done." Today Mission Bay combines a world-class interplay of research, science, and medical facilities with a residential community, all of which is set apart from the downtown congestion. It is literally next to the bay and probably enjoys the best weather in San Francisco.

Residential

Bosa Development is led by the visionary Nat Bosa and is based in Vancouver, British Columbia, where the company has built some sixty condominium towers over the last thirty years. Bosa brought the Radiance to market in 2008, just as the Financial Disaster was gathering steam.

What Salesforce.com Means to Mission Bay

Salesforce.com purchased fourteen *acres* in the heart of Mission Bay with the intention of building a two-million-square-foot campus for eight thousand plus employees.

Like many companies, Salesforce.com wanted a site where employees could be together rather than spread among many buildings.

In choosing a new HQ location, employees were asked whether they wished to be in a high-rise downtown (close to shopping and dining) or in Mission Bay. They chose Mission Bay. "There is nothing quite so inspiring to see the possibilities as an empty lot overlooking one of the most historic, wonderful bays in the universe," said Bruce Francis, Salesforce.com's vice president of corporate strategy.

Madrone Condominiums

While other developers were licking their financial wounds, Bosa started building the new 329-unit Madrone next to the existing Radiance. This was in early 2010, even before the Salesforce.com announcement; it was a gutsy move.

Great Opportunity, Tricky Market

With 329 units at the Madrone, there are many choices and an overall great opportunity. Ten years from now, Mission Bay will be "done" and will be a sought-after neighborhood just as SOMA is now sought after by tech companies and residents. However, it is a tricky market, and a buyer needs to be careful about which unit at what price represents a good deal and needs to consider the unit's configuration, available light and views, and so on.

Transbay Terminal
July 2013

Have you been watching the Transbay Terminal take shape? The project started in 2010 with the demolition of the 1939 Mission Street bus terminal. It is scheduled for completion in 2017.

Thanks to the TJPA (Transbay Joint Powers Authority), I was able to tour the site in early June. Below is a view of the site under construction, looking west from the twentieth floor of the TJPA office at 201 Mission Street. The Millennium Tower is in the right foreground, and the Black Rock building at 400 Howard Street is midframe on the left.

Below is a rendering of the 5.4-acre park that will sit atop the terminal as well as a rendering of the adjacent Cesar Pelli office tower. The images are courtesy of TJPA.

When finished, this tower will be 1,070 feet tall, making it the seventh-tallest building in the United States and twenty feet higher than New York's Chrysler Building.

The opening of AT&T Park in March 2000 was probably the single most important catalyst in transforming the neighborhoods south of Market Street. The opening of the Transbay Terminal with Pelli Tower seventeen years after the opening of AT&T Park is likely to have an even greater impact on the residential and commercial vibrancy of SOMA.

The terminal brings eleven transportation systems together under one roof. As it is LEED gold certified, it incorporates green-building strategies including solar shading, wind power, and the use of natural light to conserve water and energy. It will reduce carbon-dioxide emissions by more than thirty-six thousand tons each year from the Caltrain extension alone.

North versus South
August 2013

Question

Are condominiums more expensive (on a dollar-per-square-foot basis) in the traditionally high-end District 7 neighborhoods of the Marina, Pacific Heights, Presidio Heights, and Cow Hollow and in District 8's Nob Hill/Russian Hill, or are they more expensive in the newer neighborhoods of Yerba Buena, South Beach, and SOMA (District 9)?

Answer

For a six-month period that ended on June 30, 2013, average condominium sale prices in Nob Hill and Russian Hill were $949 per square foot versus $917 per square foot in District 7 and $895 per square foot in the south of Market neighborhoods.

Ten years ago, in 2003, condos in the District 7 neighborhoods sold at $604 per square foot and were the most expensive. Nob Hill/ Russian Hill condominiums sold for $551 per square foot, and properties in District 9 were in third place at $494 per square foot.

The High-End Is Different

At prices of more than $1 million, the story is different. For the six-month period that ended in June 2013, there were 105 sales at more than $1 million each south of Market, and they averaged $1,042 per square foot. This exceeded the 60 sales at $1,030 per square foot in Nob Hill/Russian Hill and the 101 sales in District 7 at $951 per square foot.

May I state the obvious? South of Market has come of age! South of Market condominiums have gone from being average to some of the most expensive in the city.

Behind the Numbers

Starting with the Brannan, most of the larger buildings have been developed with an amenity package not found in other parts of the city. They include air conditioning, a fitness center, a swimming pool, a concierge, key-fob security, and, in some cases, a media center. In addition, these buildings have better systems; require less maintenance; are situated in the midst of a growing list of dining options; are close to workplaces, shopping, and freeways; are mostly on flat blocks; and enjoy better weather than those on the north side do.

It is also interesting to note that south of Market buildings are generally larger than those on the north side by some 15 to 20 percent. Their HOA dues are typically lower, even though their amenities are more extensive. This is primarily because the common costs are allocated over a large number of building units.

Going Forward

Will this trend continue? Most likely. We have already seen what AT&T Park has done, and that was just thirteen years ago. Coming soon are Transbay Terminal, an underground transit system originating at Fourth and King that will facilitate travel between Silicon Valley and the city, and more commercial and residential buildings in South Mission Bay, all of which will reinforce the trend toward higher per-square-foot residential prices south of Market.

So Much!
May 2015

So much is happening in our little hamlet of San Francisco that I don't know where to start or, for that matter, to end. There are dozens of "small" condominium and apartment developments that we drive by every day. There are 20-unit developments, 200-unit developments, and even Lumina's 650-unit development downtown. The sheer size and neighborhood impact of the developments that we may not normally drive by are breathtaking.

CPMC

The new CPMC campus takes up an entire city block between Van Ness/Franklin and Geary/Post. It's a five-year build, and its completion is slated for 2019. It will include a twelve-story acute-care facility, a 274-bed patient hospital, and a nine-story medical office building. It is already influencing two condominium developments under construction close by: the 69-unit 1450 Franklin and the 260-unit Rockwell on Pine between Van Ness and Franklin.

Warriors Stadium

This twelve-acre development between Mission Bay and Dogpatch will have an eighteen-thousand-seat arena and a million square feet of commercial/industrial space, including restaurants and retail. Just as AT&T Park was a major catalyst for residential development in South Beach and SOMA, the Warriors complex is likely to influence Dogpatch, Potrero, Mission Bay, and Central Waterfront residential.

5 M

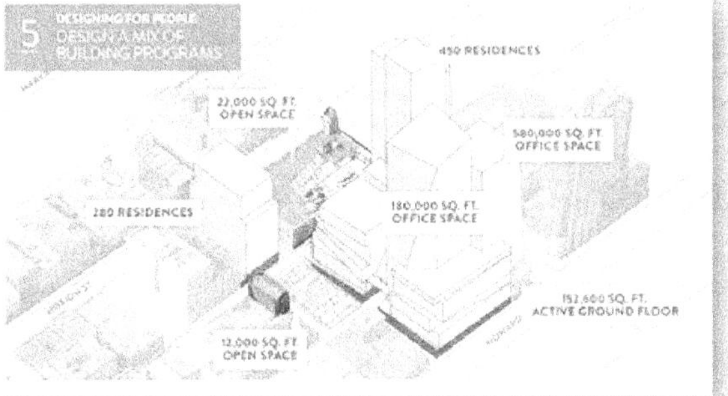

This is four acres smack in the middle of downtown. Its hub is the Chronicle Building (Fifth and Mission). As you can see from the graphic, it involves offices, retail, arts, residential buildings, and open space.

Treasure Island

This Lennar/Wilson Meany development in the middle of San Francisco Bay will take some ten years to complete and will include eight thousand homes, three hotels, 250,000 or more square feet of commercial space, its own ferry terminal, and some three hundred acres of parks and open space. The graphic is an imagined nighttime view of it from the Embarcadero. The folks who purchased units in Tower Two at the Infinity will be blessed with a spectacular nighttime vista.

Pier 70

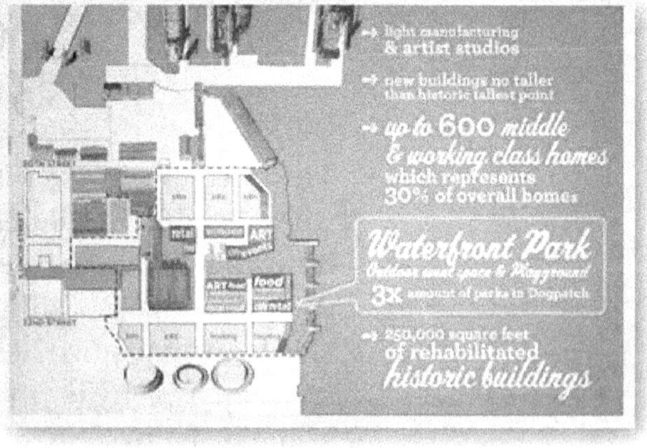

Just south of Mission Bay, Pier 70 was a shipbuilding center "turning out everything from ocean schooners, ferry boats, to warships from the Spanish-American War to Vietnam." Forest City is proposing shops, restaurants, small manufacturers, residential space, office space, and a Bayfront park on a twenty-eight-acre site.

Transbay

The price per square foot of downtown condominiums already exceeds that of other San Francisco neighborhoods, and the construction of the Transbay Terminal (a.k.a. "the Grand Central Terminal of the West") is one of the reasons. It is breathtaking in its size, grandeur, and impact on the city as a whole. Who says I can't exaggerate?

Bayview—Hunters Point

This massive twenty-year development by Lennar will have more than ten thousand residential units, two million plus square feet of office/retail space, a new stadium, three hundred plus acres of parkland, and some of the best weather in San Francisco, not to mention waterfront views. It is just three and a half miles north of AT&T Park at the southern edge of SOMA, a stone's throw from SFO, and an easy commute for those who work in Silicon Valley.

These seven developments are massive in scale, not to mention in their long-term impact on adjacent neighborhoods and on the city as a whole.

Transformation
October 2015

There seems to be a clamor among the natives that all of the construction in the city is creating monumental traffic gridlock, displacing people, and changing the face of our fair city.

Been There

Moscone Center, which was named for Mayor Moscone, who was murdered in 1978, was built in 1981, though it was initially opposed by Moscone when he served on the board of supervisors in the 1960s. He felt it would "displace elderly and poor residents of the area." It has since transformed the surrounding neighborhoods.

In 1997, UC Regents approved Mission Bay as the site for UCSF's new campus, and with Mayor Willie Brown's help, Catellus Development Corporation was "encouraged" to donate forty-three acres of property to UCSF Mission Bay. It transformed Mission Bay into a home to many of the most advanced research facilities in the world.

Then AT&T Park opened in March 2000, and besides bringing three World Series championships to the city, it transformed all of King Street and multiple blocks to the north with new housing and retail and commercial buildings.

The city is going through a growth spurt, which it does now and then. The city's population stood at 803,000 or so in 2010, having grown an average of 2,800 people each year beginning in 2000.

Since 2000, the growth has been, on average, 4,000 people a year, but lately the city has been growing at the rate of 10,000 people per year! San Francisco is the Bay Area's densest city and one of the densest in the country.

What's on Tap?

At least eight major developments are in the works, and each will have a dramatic, transformative impact on its respective neighborhood and probably on the city as a whole.

1. Transbay Terminal—downtown
2. Warriors Arena—Mission Bay
3. Pier 70—Dogpatch
4. 5 M—Fifth Street and Mission Street
5. CPMC—Van Ness, Russian Hill, Pacific Heights, and others
6. Sea Wall Lot 337—Mission Bay
7. Treasure Island—you pick it
8. Shipyard—Bayview and Hunters Point

Urbanization

Yes, the city is changing, and the old refrain about displacing the elderly and poor is once again front and center. I share these concerns. Mayor Lee spoke at the recent *Business Times* event, and I sensed that he's not only empathetic to this displacement but also has the vision, will, and political support to lessen the impact of it.

Urbanization is happening all over the world. Cities are becoming denser, and San Francisco is no exception. In 2000, we were a quaint city of 775,000 souls. By 2030, we will likely be a robust city of 1,000,000.

CHAPTER 3

The Seven Sisters and Other Buildings of Note

There are approximately three thousand condominium buildings in San Francisco with an average of fifteen units per building, so there are forty-five thousand individual condominiums.

Until 2000 and the opening of AT&T Park, there were no condominium buildings of any size south of Market Street. Then came 219 Brannan in 2001, the first of a three-building complex conceived by a New York developer.

Since that time, there have been eighty or more new condominium buildings developed in neighborhoods south of Market Street. Many of them compete with the vintage 1920s or 1930s buildings north of Market Street located in the traditionally upper-end neighborhoods of Pacific Heights, Presidio Heights, Cow Hollow, the Marina, Russian Hill, and Nob Hill.

This chapter is about these new buildings.

The Seven Sisters of San Francisco November 2009

If someone were to mention the Seven Sisters, what would come to mind? For some it would be the seven major oil companies that ruled the world before the Arab states got together and formed OPEC in 1960.

It could be the seven all-women liberal-arts colleges in the Northeast that were founded between 1837 and 1889 and remained as single-gender schools until Vassar went coed in 1969, and Radcliffe merged with Harvard in 1999.

"Seven Sisters" is the English name given to a group of Moscow skyscrapers designed in the Stalinist era and built between 1947 and 1953. They were built in an elaborate combination of Russian baroque and Gothic styles using technology employed in building American skyscrapers.

Now the world has the Seven Sisters of San Francisco, the name that I've bestowed on select high-end condominium buildings that are new to the San Francisco skyline:

1. **The Brannan** - a three-building complex started in 2001.
2. **The Four Seasons** - the city's first condominiums on top of a five-star hotel.
3. **The St. Regis** - similar to the Four Seasons hotel/condo model.

4. **The Ritz-Carlton** - a five-star hotel-brand building without the hotel.
5. **One Rincon** - a sixty-story tower that guards the Bay Bridge entrance.
6. **The Infinity** - a 650-unit complex with two towers and two podium buildings.
7. **The Millennium** - a sixty-story tower with an eleven-story podium building by the same folks who developed the Four Seasons.

Together, these seven properties contain 2,051 condominiums and offer a host of amenities that did not exist in any San Francisco residential building before 2001. San Francisco has been recognized as a world-class city for decades, but it existed without world-class condominium buildings before the Seven Sisters.

So why are these buildings dubbed the "Seven Sisters" while others are not? It has to do mostly with amenities.

Amenities

While not all of the Seven Sisters have the same amenities, they all have two things in common: central air conditioning and concierges. Many may think that air conditioning is not an amenity, but it is. While there are a number of high-end 1920s and 1930s buildings in the city, none have air conditioning, as it was not available back then. All Seven Sisters have on-site concierges and state-of-the-art security.

They all have fitness centers, and most have media rooms, wine lockers, business centers, swimming pools, and, in some cases, on-site dining.

Location

The Seven Sisters are clustered in the neighborhoods south of Market Street, although the Ritz-Carlton sits on the north side of Market Street.

Ritz-Carlton
March 2009

First we had the Four Seasons build a 277-room hotel with 142 condominiums at 765 Market Street. Marketing started at the height of the dot-com era (January 2000) and continued through the bust, and the final sale took place sixty or so months later in May 2005. Though the initial market timing was challenging, the project has been well received in recent years.

Then we had the St. Regis build a 260-room hotel at the corner of Mission and Third Street with 102 condominiums. The hotel opened in November of 2005, and as of March 2006, except for a handful of condominiums, all units had been sold.

Now here comes the Ritz-Carlton with a different and quite interesting marketing concept: condominiums, fractional ownerships, and no hotel. While Ritz-Carlton has succeeded with this concept at resort locations, this attempt in San Francisco is its first in an urban environment.

690 Market Street

Ritz-Carlton joined with developer The Hunter Group, the owner of 690 Market Street at Kearny. Built in 1890 and home to the *San Francisco Chronicle* until 1924, when it became an office building, this sixteen-story Romanesque-style building designed by Chicago architect Daniel Burnham of Burnham and Root was the city's first steel-framed skyscraper. It survived the 1906 earthquake. See the picture of the original building.

Ritz-Carlton San Francisco

There are fifty-two condominiums called "private residences" on the top twelve floors of the renovated structure at 690 Market Street. On the lower eleven floors, there are forty-nine units (averaging four to a floor) that are being sold as one-twelfth deeded fractional interests that entitle the owner to a minimum usage of twenty-one days each year, though not necessarily in the specific unit actually owned.

A fractional owner has unlimited use of the units at any Ritz-Carlton Club for about $150 per night, and instead of a three-hundred-square-foot hotel room, the owner will have access to a one-thousand-square-foot condominium. These units come with high-touch service including a concierge, well-trained staff, valet parking, preferred access to other Ritz-Carlton Clubs, and 30 percent off the rack rate of Ritz-Carlton Hotels worldwide.

Summing Up

Unlike at the Four Seasons and St. Regis developments, there is no traditional hotel at the Ritz: there are no public meeting rooms, restaurants, or bars, though a fitness facility is planned. At the Four Seasons and St. Regis, the first twenty or so floors are devoted to traditional hotel rooms; the next twenty or so stories are condominiums, some of which have pretty decent views. The Ritz-Carlton San Francisco is scheduled for occupancy in November 2007, the same time that the first tower at 300 Spear Street will be available for occupancy. At 300 Spear, you will have a thirty-five-story tower, and some of the units will have knockout bay views. Is this a different buyer than for the Ritz-Carlton? Stay tuned.

Historic image courtesy of the San Francisco Center in the San Francisco Public Library. The historic photo was taken by T. E. Hecht.

Lessons from New York
July 2006

I just returned from a trip to New York City. The main purpose was to join a ninetieth birthday celebration. So what does a San Francisco realtor do during the day? How about visiting ten new residential developments to add to one's perspective of the San Francisco real estate scene? Of course.

While I admit to being struck by some of the differences in real estate between the two cities, some basic similarities and the level of competition (there is a lot of new-unit inventory on the market) had me wondering whether some of the trends I saw in New York would occur in San Francisco. The following comments relate only to high-rise units in both cities.

New York Parking

In San Francisco it is common to ask whether parking is deeded. In New York one need not ask. Deeded parking does not exist. Owners are lucky if there's parking on site. More often, it is around the corner or down the block. Parking is typically owned and operated by an outside concessionaire, and it generally costs $500 or $600 per month, versus a leased parking cost of $250 or $300 per month in San Francisco.

Concierges, Finishes, Views, and Other Amenities

I think every development I visited plans to have a concierge. What struck me was that some concierges are being touted as better than other concierges. It is not enough these days to have a concierge; it is competitively better to have a *name* concierge who is on site twenty-four-seven rather than just a phone call away. Most buildings are also promoting their *name* architect and/or interior designer.

New York has the Empire State Building, the Chrysler Building, famous bridges of its own, and the beautiful expanse of Central Park. With the exception of buildings on Central Park South and West, particularly those units facing the park, views at other buildings are generally more pedestrian. However, they are jealously guarded. In more than one instance, I was told that the developer had purchased "air rights" of adjoining buildings to ensure that there would be no future construction that could affect the existing views and light.

Money Issues

When a property is sold in San Francisco, the seller is subject to a transfer tax of $7.50 per $1,000.00 of value, and the tax is paid to the city coffers. That is $7,500 per $1 million dollars. In New York the transfer tax is around 1.8 percent, and there is an additional "mansion tax" of 1.0 percent for properties over $1 million. This works out to a total cost of $28,000 on each $1 million. Though San Franciscans grumble about the transfer tax, we should consider ourselves lucky.

Another difference is the amount of the deposit required to reserve a new unit. If you want to reserve a unit at the new One Rincon Hill or Infinity building, you make a nonrefundable deposit of 3 to 5 percent at the time of contract. The balance is due upon delivery of the unit—that is, when it's ready for occupancy. In New York you're required to come up with 10 percent upon signing of the contract and an additional 10 to 15 percent some four to eight months in the future. This creates more of a disincentive to walking away from the transaction.

Buyer Motivations

Though new buildings generally don't have the charm of those built in the 1920s or the 1930s, many do have spacious rooms, generous closet space, and good flow. They have updated systems and appliances and usually have fewer maintenance issues. I wonder whether some owners in classic Pacific Heights, Nob Hill, and Russian Hill buildings will opt for new homes in the south of Market towers. Some have already done this with purchases at the Four Seasons, St. Regis, and Ritz-Carlton properties. I'd bet that more will too.

Being Big Has Its Issues
September 2006

As we all know, there has been a lot of buzz about One Rincon and the Infinity. I've been thinking about these large projects within the context of the south of Market landscape and the confines of the San Francisco residential market as a whole.

Think About the Exit

Each condominium buyer has his or her special reason for buying. The thought of selling doesn't typically enter the buyer's consciousness at the time of purchase.

However, the larger the building, the less control an owner may have over the outcome at the time of the sale.

The What's-Going-to-Happen Issue

I had a client from the East Bay who was looking for a pied-à-terre in the city. He and his wife wanted a location downtown and close to BART. Views were not important. I found that 199 New Montgomery fit the bill. In preparation for a Sunday tour, I did a little research and found that there were six units listed. I thought that that was good, since it would give my client an opportunity to compare layouts and outlooks.

As a well-informed broker, I know that there are always factors that I don't even know that I don't know about! When I talked with one of the listing agents, I learned something unexpected. There were seventeen units still owned by the developer, and they were being fed into the market as current leases expired and market conditions allowed them to be sold. I thought the building was "sold out," and I guess that you could say it was. In a more practical sense, it was not.

Coincidentally, two days before my tour, I talked with a friend who'd bought a unit at 199 New Montgomery and then moved into a different building. The last time we talked, she told me that she placed her unit at 199 New Montgomery on the market to sell. When I chatted with her last week, she said in a frustrated tone, "There are always six units on the market, and I got frustrated trying to sell mine, so I just decided to rent it." When I asked whether she knew of the seventeen developer units, she said, "Wow, I didn't know."

The Competitive Landscape Issue

The buildings built between 2000 and 2005 are subject to more competitive pressures from the newer buildings nearby—One Rincon, the Infinity, and their sisters still on the drawing boards. If I were an owner at 199 New Montgomery, the Brannan, or Bridgeview, I would be competing with other sellers in my building and with those in the newer building as well. This is already happening.

Those who bought at The Metropolitan should have known of the future competitive landscape down the road when they made that decision. The information is widely available if you know where to look. And should I buy at One Rincon, the Infinity, or the upcoming developments on Fremont, Mission, or Folsom, I should have an eye toward future competition as well.

Some Hidden Issues

Both One Rincon and the Infinity are now asking buyers to enter into contracts to purchase property in anticipation of occupancy that may not occur until the fourth quarter of 2007 or sometime in early 2008. Buyers need to check whether their contracts are assignable in the event that their circumstances change.

I have not reviewed all of the documents, but it is highly unlikely that these contracts are assignable, which means that a buyer might forfeit the 3 to 5 percent deposit should he or she opt out of the contract. This may be real money to some, and it's the price of changing one's mind.

And then there are the restrictions on the ability to sell after close of escrow. There may be restrictions that preclude you from selling within the first year after closing. There also may be a clause that requires you to give the developer a right of first refusal until his entire development has been sold out.

Here we are in mid-2006, and unit delivery and occupancy may not take place until the fourth quarter of 2007 or even the first quarter of 2008. Buyers may not be able to sell independently of the developer until 2009 or 2011. Hmm.

Summing Up

Buyers are choosing the south of Market neighborhoods because of their location and attractive amenities. These are good buildings with lots of pluses: some are in walking distance to the Financial

District, BART, Union Square, restaurants, or the Embarcadero, and some have physical-fitness amenities, concierges, or good views.

Despite these attributes, many of the owners and would-be sellers of existing units may be disappointed that they're unable to sell their units when they desire to sell them. This inability to sell is not the result of increased interest rates or other economic factors but of in-building competition as well as competition from new buildings nearby.

So the takeaway for would-be buyers is to be aware of all of the potential issues concerning selling when you're thinking about making the decision to buy.

New Sister in Town: The Millennium November 2007

Periodically, a new sister building comes to town and causes quite a stir. Last year two new sisters, One Rincon and the Infinity, graced our stage, imposing their towering heights and plentiful amenities on San Francisco. While the Millennium (301 Mission Street) is statuesque in her own right, she brings some new qualities to the residential party here in San Francisco.

When complete, the Millennium will be 647 feet tall and will have a total of 419 condominium units compared to the 709 units at the two Rincon towers and the 650 units at the Infinity.

Revealing

A classic striptease artist never reveals everything at once. After all, it is about the thrill of anticipation. The normal marketing routine involves releasing only a portion of the units, evaluating the market's response, and then releasing additional units in phases, increasing the prices in a rising market.

Not so with the Millennium. She is revealing it all. There are three distinct product segments in this development, and all of them are for sale. Occupancy is expected in spring 2009. This difference in marketing tactics is based on the Millennium's differentiating between the products it offers, which are three distinct luxury products. By doing so, they are betting that they'll gain more from making all of the units available at the outset than they would from learning from the market response and increasing prices over time. My bet is that they know what they're doing. After all, they developed the city's first mixed-use luxury development, the Four Seasons Hotel and Residences on Market Street in 2001, plus they've built Ritz-Carlton and Four Seasons hotels in other markets, including in New York, Boston, and Washington, DC.

There are no walk-ins allowed. That's right—you can't just drop into the sales office and eat up the time of the small, select sales staff. This may make some prospective buyers unhappy, but I think that it sets a good initial screening process for qualifying buyers. This is not a development with low-, medium-, and high-end units. They are all expensive.

Product Segmentation

There are three product segments within the Millennium complex: one is an eleven-story podium building with fifty-three homes called "City Residences." They are all one-bedroom units, the smallest of which is 1,280 square feet and the largest of which is 2,280 square feet. They will catch the eye of the market, where the average size of a one-bedroom unit is 800 square feet!

Then there's the tower: it has 191 units called the "Residences" on floors three to twenty-five with 9 units on each floor. The Grand Residences are on floors twenty-six to sixty and total 175 units.

There are only 6 units per floor up to the forty-eighth floor, and then there are only 4 units per floor from the forty-ninth to the fifty-eighth floor. There are two penthouses on both the fifty-ninth and sixtieth floors that are being sold as shell space.

Each of the three segments of the Millennium has its own lobby, its own homeowners association, and its own concierges.

Amenity Floor (Club Level)

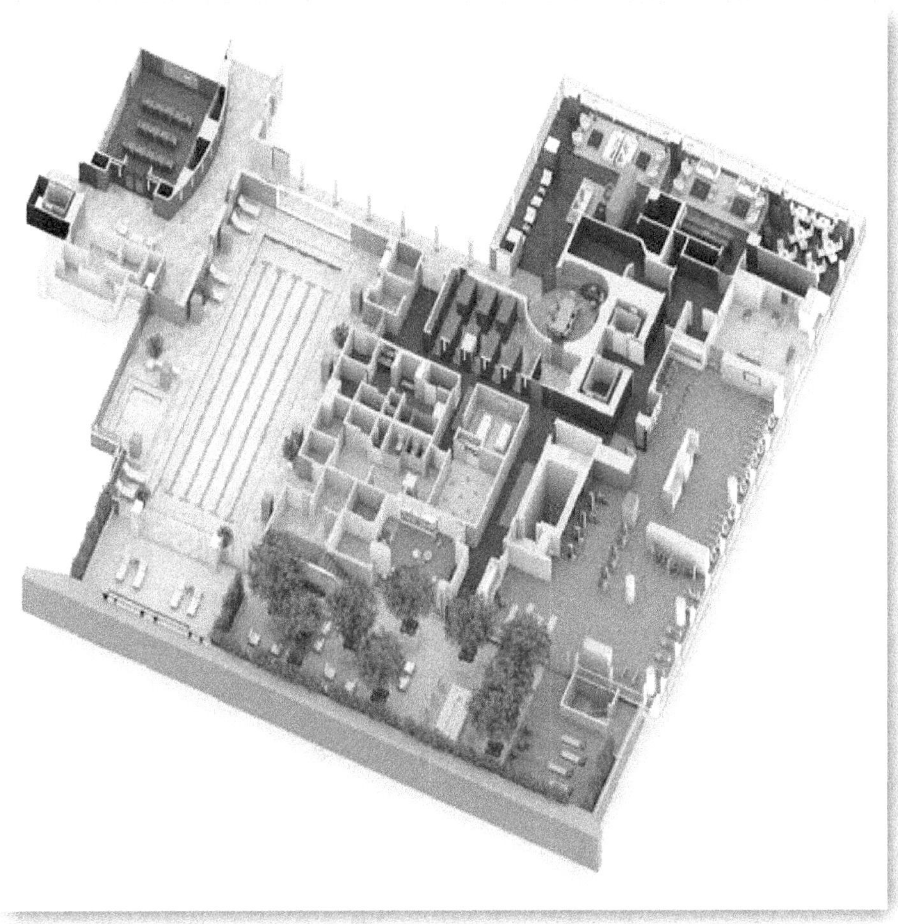

The rendering depicts the planned twenty-thousand-square-foot "club level" that features an owners-only dining room; an owners lounge with an adjacent wine cellar and tasting room; a screening room; a children's playroom; an outdoor terrace; and a Sports Club/LA–managed fifty-five-hundred-square-foot fitness center that includes Pilates and yoga studios, locker rooms, Jacuzzi and steam rooms, and a seventy-five-foot indoor swimming pool. The scope and size of this club level dwarfs that of any other condominium or hotel facility in the city. There will also be a Michael Minna wine-themed restaurant at the bottom of the building (Mission Street and Fremont Street) open to the public.

View, Location, Service, and Amenities

The three largest condominium developments in San Francisco, One Rincon, the Infinity, and the Millennium, are all attractive and innovative in different ways. However, as time goes on, I think each will become known in the marketplace by its most distinctive feature. One Rincon, which sits at the highest point of Rincon Hill, is principally about views. It sacrifices location to some extent by being on First Street and the entrance to the Bay Bridge.

The Infinity is about location, which is probably the best of any of the new developments. It's one block from the Embarcadero and on Folsom Street, which will eventually become a retail/pedestrian boulevard.

The Millennium will be distinguished by its service, extensive amenities, and club facilities. Its multiple concierges will exceed anything else in the city. It's estimated that it will have a staff of forty-five people, including concierges, parking valets, door attendants, engineers, security, and a full-time cleaning staff. It will offer a level of service and amenities normally found in a five-star hotel.

Summing Up

The Millennium is making a bold statement: this is where you want to be—if you can afford it. The Millennium is the new sister in town, and for now, it's the most elegant. It is hitting the market during a national housing crisis. Because it's aimed at the high end, it may not experience a bump in the road. That won't be the case for the fifteen or so other new developments now selling units or about to come to market in 2008.

The good news is that with all of the new developments south of Market, there are multiple choices. The Millennium is not for everyone, even at the upper end of the market. The Four Seasons, St. Regis, Infinity, One Rincon, Radiance, and Ritz-Carlton all have their pluses. The bad news is that whether you're at the low end, in the middle, or at the high end, it takes research and expertise to evaluate the opportunities that exist, compare their pluses and minuses, and then make an informed decision to suit your current and long-term needs.

It's Not Complicated
March 2010

While single-family homeowners can control their own property costs, condominium buyers are often in the dark when it comes to what's covered by monthly HOA dues and whether dues will be increased in the future. Monthly dues vary widely for a number of reasons.

Consider the average monthly HOA dues for six of the Seven Sisters. The first column shows average monthly dues on a per-square-foot basis, and the second column shows the monthly dollar cost applied to a same-sized 1,500-square-foot unit.

	Average cost per square foot	Cost for a 1,500-square-foot unit
Ritz-Carlton	$1.58	$2,370.00
Four Seasons	$1.35	$2,025.00
St. Regis	$1.27	$1,905.00
The Brannan	$0.77	$1,155.00
One Rincon	$0.65	$ 975.00
The Infinity	$0.54	$ 810.00

Why is there such a difference? All of these buildings have similar amenities—a concierge, on-site security, a fitness center, a swimming pool (except the Ritz-Carlton), parking, air conditioning, and professional management. Apart from possible differences in concierge service levels, there are at least three or more reasons that account for the substantial difference in monthly costs, not only with these select buildings but also for all condominium buildings.

Size Matters

There are two categories of costs that make up the basis for monthly HOA dues: normal operating costs (common-area utilities, maintenance, building insurance, garbage removal, etc.), and a reserve fund to cover anticipated major capital items (re-roofing, painting, elevator overhaul, etc.). The aggregate of these costs is divided among the owners to calculate monthly HOA dues per owner.

For the Brannan, One Rincon, and the Infinity, the costs are allocated between 339, 390, and 650 owners, respectively. For the Ritz-Carlton, Four Seasons, and the St. Regis, the denominators are 101, 142, and 102, respectively.

The smaller the number of owners, the higher the share of the dues.

Valet Parking

If there is one parking space per owner, each owner is able to self-park. Otherwise, a valet is needed to park the owners' cars. Valet parking is an incremental operating expense, and it is borne by the HOA. The Brannan and the Infinity have deeded parking. The others employ a valet service, which increases respective monthly dues (and may not be included in the stated HOA dues number).

Earthquake Insurance

It's expensive, and most HOA Boards conclude that it is not cost-effective. The Four Seasons and the St. Regis HOAs pay for earthquake insurance coverage because they are part of a hotel complex, and hotel lenders demand it. The Ritz-Carlton also carries earthquake insurance. The others do not.

Special Assessments

Special assessments are levied when unanticipated (major) costs arise. Often an assessment is used to remediate a major water leak or a major system failure. However, sometimes it is quite different. In the case of the Ritz-Carlton, an assessment that resulted from "seismic safety improvements" done by the developer was placed on the owners' shoulders. The developer created a $30 million thirty-year bond obligation to offset a portion of the development expenses. The bonds were sold to investors and were to be paid back with interest over time.

Some of the original Ritz-Carlton buyers claimed that there was not adequate notification at the time of purchase, and they litigated the bonds. This assessment is in the form of a Mello-Roos tax and is part of the property tax statement. In effect, the city is the assessment collector. The obligation has another twenty-eight years to run.

So if you were to buy at the Ritz Carlton, you might be obligated to pay $6.50 per square foot per year or more for the next twenty-eight years. For a 1,500-square-foot unit, that would be $273,000 over twenty-eight years—which is something to keep in mind.

Bottom Line

It is worth taking the time to understand what goes into the calculation of the HOA dues. After all, these dues are not tax deductible.

They can also become an impediment to selling one's condominium or at the very least can result in a seller receiving a reduced price when there is a large, unanticipated special assessment. It's really not that complicated, but caveat emptor.

Note that the Millennium is one of the Seven Sisters and has two buildings and three homeowner associations. Its dues are a bit complicated. The monthly HOA dues for the "Residences" range from \$0.51 per square foot to \$1.17 per square foot. The "Grand Residences'" HOA dues range from \$0.41 per square foot to \$0.86 per square foot, and those of the "City Residences" range from \$0.80 per square foot to \$1.04 per square foot.

Seven Sisters Update
February 2011

A year ago, on February 18, I hosted thirty-five Bay Area agents for a half-day visit to three upper-end residential buildings in San Francisco's south of Market Street neighborhood. We started with a visit to 5304 at One Rincon Hill, followed that with lunch at 41B in Tower Two at the Infinity, and finished with coffee and dessert at the Millennium sales office.

During my opening remarks, I mentioned that there was $500 million of available inventory in these three buildings. Here we are a year later.

One Rincon Hill, with a total of 390 units, had roughly 80 units for sale last year at this time. Unit 5304, where we started our tour with champagne and hors d'oeuvres, was listed for $2,865,000. Today there are fewer than 35 unsold units, and 5304 is still available and is now listed for $2,640,000.

We had lunch at 41B at the Infinity (which has 650 units in four buildings). In February 2010, there were 40 units available. Unit 41B was listed then for $7,350,000; today it is available for $5,100,000. It has unobstructed views of the bay and the Bay Bridge and dead-on Treasure Island views that will only get better, particularly at nighttime, when Treasure Island is developed.

We finished up at the Millennium (419 units). In February 2010 about one-quarter of the building had been sold. Today almost half of the units have been sold.

One Rincon Hill

Infinity

Millennium

What about the other Seven Sisters?

Both 2009 and 2010 were difficult years for the residential real estate market, as you know. Although we suffered in San Francisco, we suffered far less than those in many other parts of the Bay Area or the country in general. Though One Rincon Hill, the Infinity, and the Millennium are too new for us to assess their overall performance, we do have some data on the other Seven Sisters since 2007, the height of the market.

The Four Seasons condominiums have held value the best, declining only 4 percent from 2007 through 2010 on an average dollars-per-square-foot basis. Unit prices at the St. Regis declined about 23 percent from 2007 through 2010, while Brannan prices declined an average of 20 percent. There were too few sales at the Ritz-Carlton for us to make any meaningful assessment of it. The superior performance of the Four Seasons is probably a result of its being the first high-end hotel with condominiums in the city and its ability to attract a more established clientele, which ensures that it experiences fewer turnovers than the others.

In Other News

Without fanfare or public announcement, Bosa Development has commenced construction on the second phase of Radiance condominiums in Mission Bay.

I suspect that they'll start their marketing in early 2012. Also in early 2012, Tishman Speyer will break ground at the southwest corner of Main and Folsom, which is currently used as a U.S. Postal Service parking lot. The development will include another 650 units and will be similar to the Infinity. The One Rincon Hill folks are a bit further behind in starting the construction of their second tower.

These three developments will add about 1,350 new units to the existing inventory of some ten thousand condominiums south of Market Street.

DOWNTOWN JULY 2012

Before moving to San Francisco, I lived in LA for twenty years, and no one ever went to downtown LA (DTLA) for anything other than business. Now it is cool!

Our downtown expanse is affectionately referred to as SOMA (south of Market Street), as opposed to the Financial District, which is north of Market Street. SOMA began its major transformation with the opening of AT&T Park in March 2000. The first residential tower at 219 Brannan started sales in the summer of 2000 with initial prices as low as $400 per square foot.

The Next Wave

The revitalization of downtown is happening all over the country—that is, a lot of people are moving back into the city. There is a real desire to have interaction with others and to not be isolated. Nobody wants to stay in their car and commute and pollute anymore. All of that is true, of course, except for young couples who leave San Francisco and must commute and pollute on behalf of their children, who need an education, but we will leave that for another *Pulse* and another day.

With the exception of Bosa's Madrone in Mission Bay, there hasn't been any construction of a major condominium building in the last couple of years. Only this last year has financing become available for apartment buildings, and while apartments "pencil," condominiums don't. I understand that Nat Bosa used his firm's own equity to launch the 329-unit Madrone, which was a gutsy and successful decision.

One Rincon Tower Two broke ground in June. It will be fifty stories when completed, compared to Tower One's sixty stories, and will contain 299 units, versus Tower One's 385 units. It is being developed as an apartment complex with a condominium map, meaning that units can be sold as condominiums in the future.

Across from Rincon Tower is 45 Lansing, which is expected to be thirty-nine stories and 320 units. The site was previously owned by Turnberry Associates. They lost the property during the great recession, and it is now being developed by Crescent Heights, the folks who brought us the Metropolitan.

Next up will likely be 201 Folsom, the parcel on the west side of Main Street across from Tishman Speyer's 650-unit Infinity. Tishman is also the developer of 201 Folsom, which will have 600 or more units.

This image shows a rendering of 201 Folsom on the right and the Infinity 301 Main Street tower on the left.
There are three more developments likely in the next wave: 399 Fremont, 706 Mission, and 8 Washington.

The first, 399 Fremont, was called "The Californian" when entitled by Chicago's Fifield during the last wave. It now has a new developer, Oliver McMillan of San Diego. It will probably be built as an apartment complex with a condominium map. The image shows the 399 Fremont tower on the left and One Rincon on the right.

Next on the list is 706 Mission, across from the St. Regis at Mission Street and Third Street. It will be a while—probably three or four years—until groundbreaking. The developer is Millennium Partners, who successfully built the Four Seasons Hotel and, more recently, the Millennium.

Summary

The first wave produced some ten thousand condominium units in SOMA, representing about 25 percent of San Francisco's condominium stock today. My sense is that the second wave will produce a more modest number and will take longer than ten years.

There seems to be little doubt that San Francisco residential real estate has rebounded better than that of any other major city in the United States. As you probably know, commercial real estate prices downtown have soared in the last twenty-four months, apartment rents continue to escalate, residential home prices have recovered from their depths (although they are still back at 2005 levels), and the tech economy is in full bloom.

Prices will recover to their 2007/2008 peaks; we just don't know when.

New Sisters
March 2014

Arden, Lumina, and Park 181 are the next condominium developments of major size and Seven Sister–like quality.

Park 181, a.k.a. 181 Fremont, is the first development by Jay Paul Company in San Francisco. It is located on Fremont just north of Howard and just behind one of my favorite restaurants, Town Hall.

It is also the first building to combine condominiums (seventy-four) on the upper fifteen floors of a fifty-four-story building with commercial tenants on the lower thirty-nine floors.

Lumina, which is at the corner of Folsom and Main, is Tishman Speyer's second residential development in San Francisco. It follows on the heels of Infinity. It will have two towers, two podium buildings, and a total of 656 units.

Arden in South Mission Bay, which has 263 units, is the third residential development by Nat Bosa, who is based in Vancouver. His first San Francisco development, Radiance, was a moderate success that had unfortunate market timing; his second, Madrone, was a smash with exquisite timing, and I expect that his third, Arden, will be a smash as well, given the robust nature of the current market demand. When he's finished, Bosa will have added

690 units in three developments to the San Francisco condominium population.

The tentative schedule is as follows:

	Sales Office Opens	Occupancy
Arden	Q 2 of 2014	Q 3 of 2015
Lumina	Q 3 of 2014	Q 2 of 2015
Park 181	Q 2 of 2015	Q 1 of 2016

Numbers

These three new developments, all of which are south of Market Street, will add only 993 condominiums to the city's housing stock over a period of about two years. Another 560 units in smaller developments are also under construction south of Market Street and should have occupancy before the end of 2015.

There are about 740 units in ten developments under construction north of Market Street. They will all be finished before the end of 2015. These developments together total 2,300 units; there will be roughly 1,150 new units per year, which is not enough to satisfy market demand.

Know the Market October 2014

New in town is Lumina by Tishman Speyer. Its launch reminds me of Alibaba's hyped IPO, which, by the way, was the same week that Lumina opened its sales office. So should we buy Alibaba stock? Should we buy a condominium at Lumina? It helps to focus on a few key issues and to know the condominium market south of Market Street.

Five years ago I coined the phrase, "the Seven Sisters of San Francisco." When comparing Lumina to other options, it's good to look at the Four Seasons, the St. Regis, the Millennium Tower, the Infinity, and the other "sisters."

Amenities

Lumina is an upscale version of its sister, the Infinity: it has two towers and two podium buildings, it's in the same location, and it has the same number of units. It has a more extensive amenity package—a BBQ pit, a climbing wall, outdoor movie screenings, pet grooming, a concierge, a members lounge, a fitness center, a lap pool, and a gourmet market—to attract the twenty- to thirtysomethings, the sixty- to seventysomethings, and the "in betweeners."

Location

Take your choice. Where do you want to be? Market Street (Four Seasons), on the edge of Yerba Buena Garden/Moscone (St. Regis), on the edge of the new Transbay Terminal (Millennium), or closer to the Embarcadero/bay? Keep in mind that 181 Fremont will also be on the edge of Transbay Terminal. Coming soon are 706 Mission at Third Street (Millennium Partners) and 160 Folsom at Main Street (Tishman).

Views

Views are very important to some people and not so important to others. The best water views are probably from the upper floors of Infinity Tower Two on Spear Street, where it is unlikely that another building will ever affect existing views.

In another vein, 706 Mission is going through litigation with some folks at the Four Seasons who feel that their existing views (and light) will be impacted by this planned forty-seven-story building. When 160 Folsom is built, it will block some existing views at both Infinity and Lumina, and Lumina will block some views at the Infinity, and vice versa. It's good to know what's coming down the pike.

Pricing

We all know that the market is hot. Tishman's market timing is quintessential. The hype is on, and available inventory is low. Keep in mind, however, that there are 656 units to sell. Sales velocity is a key metric for developers.

Bargain in Our Midst
January 2015

What?

There are 182 homes (dubbed Summit 800) under construction on the western edge of the city; one-third of them are single-family homes, one-third of them are town homes, and one-third are condominiums. All of them are three-bedroom, two-and-a-half-bathroom units. They range in size from 1,500 square feet to 2,100 square feet and are priced between $650 per square foot and $850 per square foot, which is a handsome value when compared to new-condominium construction in other areas of the city where prices often exceed $1,100 per square foot.

The layouts are very thoughtful, the finishes are attractive, and the units have spacious garages, low HOA dues, and good outlooks. The builder is Comstock Homes, based in Manhattan Beach, California. I believe that this is their first foray into the San Francisco market. Hats off to them.

Why?

San Francisco housing is now ridiculously expensive, and yet it "pays" to be in the city! This development offers an opportunity to get into the game at a reasonable price. For someone currently paying $3,000 to $4,000 a month in rent, assuming a 20 percent down payment and low interest rates, how could one not purchase one of these homes in the $1.3 to $1.5 million range?

Where?

That's the key question. The developer has carved a new street (Summit Way) off of Brotherhood Way.

Ever wonder why there is a San Francisco street named Brotherhood Way? I never did, but on my way to play golf at Harding Park, I became curious about why there were so many religious schools and churches on this one street. Brotherhood Way was the creation of former Mayor George Christopher, who in 1958 sold surplus land on the south side of what is now Brotherhood Way to a variety of religious institutions. The street was renamed in honor of the ecumenical religious mix. Who knew?

Who?

This development makes sense for someone who needs space at a reasonable price, someone who rents, and/or someone who would like to be near 280 so that he or she can get to Palo Alto and Menlo Park in about thirty minutes, to Mission Bay and AT&T Park in about fifteen minutes, or to GGB and UCSF Parnassus via Nineteenth Avenue in about twenty minutes. Though this location is great for those people, a drawback is that there is no walkable neighborhood. Can't have everything!

CHAPTER 4

Insights, Perspectives, and Other Residential Real Estate Issues

This chapter is about various subjects that don't easily fall into one of the previous three chapters, and yet each of these *Pulses* will add to your chances of making better residential decisions. The chapter touches on issues that you may not have considered and on ones that may seem relatively minor but may in fact have a significant impact on your life.

Changing Lifestyle Needs
October 2004

We typically check the makeup of our stock-and-bond portfolio as we go through life, making adjustments for risk tolerance, our changing financial condition, and our family situation. Why not do the same with our residential real estate as our age and lifestyle change?

Buyers typically buy real estate because they no longer want to rent, they're relocating, they need more space for a growing family, they can afford a larger and/or more conveniently located home, or for other reasons. A sale typically takes place because of a need to relocate and/or downsize, a divorce, or a death in the family.

But there are a host of other reasons for buying and selling that are directly related to the natural aging process.

Steps and Hills

I have a cousin in Atlanta, an orthopedic surgeon who performs 450 total-joint replacement operations a year. He is often on my mind. So when I have a conversation with a client who lives with his wife on the top floor of a multi-unit building in Pacific Heights—one that has to have sixty or more steps to the front door—and he tells me that he's in the preliminary stages of renovating the building and combining the top two floors for himself and his wife, I think of hip and knee replacements. I can't help but be sensitive to what I perceive to be my clients' needs, even though my clients may not acknowledge them.

Steps are not a small issue. I count steps when I go on Tuesday broker tours; fifteen steps are ok, but when you get north of thirty steps, there's a problem, not only for those of us with gray hair but also for young parents with babies and groceries in tow.

In the same vein, a flat block is often preferable to a hilly block. Hills are an issue in tony Pacific Heights, Russian Hill, and Nob Hill and in other neighborhoods. They are not an issue in the Marina, South Beach, SOMA, and Mission Bay.

Travel and Security

I have clients who travel quite a bit, and because they're security conscious, they no longer wish to maintain a single-family home and to concern themselves with security issues while away. A doorman building, a key-operated elevator, an on-site manager, and other such amenities ease security concerns.

Above and Below the Line

When advising buyers, I suggest that they draw an imaginary horizontal line across an imaginary piece of paper. I ask them to place two or three items above the line that are absolutely essential; everything else goes below the line. As our lifestyles change, the importance of any one issue also changes. When we're in our twenties and thirties, steps, hills, and doormen may be less important than they are when we're in our sixties and seventies. While we may have been willing to live without a view for twenty or thirty years, we may really want a view when we return to our home in San Francisco after a long trip. Our wants and needs change!

The Buy Side Increasing the Odds May 2005

As an example, I'll talk about a recent buy offer. It was a two-bedroom, one-bath upper unit in a two-unit building with one-car parking. The list price was $840,000. I always encourage my buyer clients to offer an aggressive price that they're "comfortable" with. And it needs to be a clean offer—that is, one with few or no contingencies. Most competent agents do the same. So how do I differentiate my clients' offer from others' offers? The differences are often in the details and nuances, just like with everything else in life.

No one is able to know how high the offer price needs to be. My goal is not to submit the highest offer price. My goal is simply to get "a second bite of the apple"—that is, to get the listing agent to either call or give me a written counteroffer. In this particular situation, I received a telephone call. The agent told me that she was giving me the courtesy call that I had requested in my cover memo, in which I'd written, "If this offer does not exactly fulfill all the needs of your sellers, please call me."

Prior to making an offer, my clients had done a property inspection, and, of course, they had obtained a preapproval letter from a lender. I was confident that the property would be appraised for the price that they were offering, so there was no finance or appraisal contingency. And we were ready to close in fifteen days.

Here's what may have made the difference: Offers were to be dropped off at the listing agent's office at a specified time and date. I asked for the opportunity to present my offer directly to the listing agent and her clients, who were meeting at the agent's office. At that meeting I made a personal contact with the sellers so that my clients' offer was not just one of six offers in a pile of papers. My flesh and blood, face, and personality became part of the equation. When the agent and her clients reviewed the six offers, our price was the second highest. Because I'd made a personal appearance, I received my "courtesy call," and by adding $20,000 to sweeten the pot (just 2.1 percent more than our original offer), we won the deal. As some wise man once said, "You need to ask for what you want." In this case, I wanted a second bite of the apple.

TO BE THIRTYSOMETHING AGAIN AND TO LIVE IN SAN FRANCISCO JULY 2005

I find it interesting that I now have a much longer time perspective than I ever had when I was thirty. Though I am older, I am now much more comfortable looking out twenty and thirty years as it relates to real estate. In the midst of the constant drumbeat of real estate–bubble mania, I can help my clients gain valuable perspective and make sounder financial decisions.

So here's a case story.

Looking at the Long Term

Here's a conundrum that we would all like to have: There's a home on the market for $4 million that my clients think is perfect for their needs. They're not sure how high of an offer to make. Like all clients, they don't want to overpay. They have a young, growing family, and they view this property as a home for the next twenty-five years.

Since 1987, the average annual appreciation of single-family homes in San Francisco has been about 7.0 percent. There was a period from 1990 to1994 when average prices actually declined, and in one year—1991—they declined by as much as 4.5 percent. In the year 2000, average prices appreciated 30.2 percent, which was an anomaly. Is it safe to say that prices will appreciate an average of

7.0 percent over the next ten or twenty years? Not really, but I would be comfortable predicting that they'll appreciate at least 2.5 percent and more than 5.0 percent on average.

If my clients make an offer of $4.5 million (12.5 percent more than the asking price), will they be overpaying? Not if they'll be staying there for the next twenty-five years—or even for ten years, for that matter.

Wrapping 2005
November 2005

To state the obvious, people are always going to be buying and selling residential real estate in San Francisco. It is always a good time to buy for those who intend to stay here (read, for at least three to five years) for the simple reason that we are a peninsula measuring seven by seven miles, and there is no place to build, with the exception of south of Market Street. One of our constants is that our real estate market is supply constrained and always will be. A second constant is that it is one hell of a great place to live.

It's not about whether this or that time is a good time to sell or buy—it's about selling and buying according to one's lifestyle and needs and then executing the process with diligence and expert advice.

It pays to make significant investment decisions tempered by careful analysis and data rather than trying to outguess the emotional ebbs and flows that make good news with the media. Now and then I run into a financially savvy client who works in the securities industry and tells me that he can earn more on his money in the stock or bond market than he can in real estate and that he's therefore in no hurry to buy a home for the family. From an overly simplistic view, this type of client has a point. But when taking into account the tax advantages and financial leverage of buying a home, the story is more telling. Savvy real estate investing is hard to beat.

Let's assume that you buy a $1 million property with 20 percent down and take out an $800,000 loan. At an annual appreciation rate of 5 percent (for the last twenty years, it has been 7 percent), the property will appreciate to $1.7 million by 2015. So your equity of $200,000 will grow to $900,000 over the span of ten years. That's $90,000 a year on a $200,000 "investment," or some 45 percent a year. Hmm.

Trusted Lender
September 2008

First, my son called me in June. He had looked into buying a condominium in Laguna Niguel for about $440,000 in the spring of 2007. He actually made an offer at the time, and for a reason I can't recall, the deal didn't go through.

Fast-forward to June of this year, and he's looking at a similar condominium, a bank foreclosure priced at $285,000, and "it's going to be competitive, Dad." He made an offer at $310,000, it was accepted, and I put him in the hands of one of my favorite San Francisco–based lender for the simple reason that I didn't want him to show up to close only to be told that the lender wouldn't perform for one reason or another. It is happening a lot. Lenders always drive the process, and at times like the present, they drive it in spades!

All went well. The appraisal came in at the $310,000 price, but the appraiser noted that the property was in a "declining market." What, pray tell, does that mean? Well, what it means is that the bank will still lend on the property but at 85 percent, not at the planned 90 percent. Okay, so we agree to put up a larger down payment. Then ten days later, our lender calls to say that the policy has changed (again) and that they will gladly lend 90 percent. A lucky break?

The moral of this story is this: make sure that you use a trusted and competent lending professional. I don't know what can go wrong, but I do know that I have a much better chance of resolving an issue if I have vetted the lender. A lender has a better chance of knowing what's about to happen when he or she is personally connected to the decision-making process within the institution (rather than with a mortgage broker). He or she is also in a position to move more swiftly and to pull things together, as happened with my son.

Waiting for Godot
January 2009

It is amazing how many would-be buyers are waiting around to buy a property. They are waiting for either the market to bottom out or for more clarity about whether the stock, bond, or real estate market will totally go to hell.

I started thinking back to my freshman-in-college days and to a play that I never really understood, Samuel Beckett's *Waiting for Godot*, which follows two consecutive days in the lives of a pair of men who divert themselves with various things and people while waiting expectantly and unsuccessfully for someone named Godot to arrive. They claim him as an acquaintance but in fact hardly know him, eventually admitting that they would not recognize him were they to see him.

I like the last part about not recognizing him were they to see him. I haven't found people who say that they'll recognize the bottom of the market when it comes, and yet they continue to wait for it.

A developer friend said it well: "It is very tough out there—nobody wants to do anything. Sellers do not want to cut prices, and buyers insist on a 'deal' to get motivated."

But will either group recognize what they're waiting for when it arrives? Everyone seems to be waiting for the real estate version of Godot. Buyers and sellers create market value through their actions. When they choose not to act, they are simply waiting to change their minds. "I have seen the enemy, and he is me."

If a buyer is planning to live in a home for the next five to ten years, this is a perfect time to purchase, given all of the waiting and hesitancy in the market. These buyers will have less competition when making an offer and will probably be able to pressure sellers on price due to the current economic circumstances.

Robin Redbreasts and Value
February 2009

You are not going to see any mention of this in the *Chronicle*, but a couple of robins have been spotted. To wit, a condominium on Russian Hill listed for $1.125 million had five offers and went into contract within forty-eight hours. A single-family home in the Marina that was originally listed for $5.4 million on August 8 was then reduced to $4.85 million sixty days later in October and to $4.5 million in mid-November, and it received four offers over the holidays and closed on January 20. Did those four buyers all go to the same New Year's Eve party and drink from the same punch bowl?

One can't blame would-be real estate buyers for being a bit nervous when both Citigroup's and Bank of America's stocks decline 20 percent and 29 percent, respectively, on Inauguration Day, and then both rebound 31 percent the very next day. "Honey, we lost our down payment on Tuesday, but we got it back on Wednesday." Right!

Let's Talk about Comps

The proverbial "comps" that most people rely on are highly suspect and may even be counterproductive if one pays attention to sale prices without understanding their context. Comps don't tell you about the nature of specific transactions or about whether more than one offer was considered at the same time. Those factors make a big difference.

The value or worth of a property is not a fixed number, contrary to what the media, as well as many buyers and sellers, may think. It's not like the bid-ask mechanism of the securities markets. When those buyers and sellers come together in a specific trade, together they establish the value of the security at that particular moment. The real estate world is much less liquid and very different.

On the Subject of Market Bottom(s)

For the $4.5 million single-family home in a certain neighborhood and at its specific price point, the market has bottomed as far as these buyers are concerned. Perhaps more importantly, they now own the home that they wanted, and the sellers sold the property that they needed to sell.

Sometimes we confuse "the news" with our news, which is a very personalized slice of reality. Relying on pundits to tell us what to do or when to buy is only one option; the other is to take back our lives and make choices based on our actual situation.

The robins are out there if you take the time to notice them, but you need to go outside and look closely to see them.

AFTERSHOCKS MAY 2009

In October 2008, I wrote a *Pulse* called "A 9.0 Worldwide Earthquake! San Francisco Survives." The following is an excerpt from it: "Folks, we just had the equivalent of a 9.0 financial earthquake, this one with an epicenter in New York City and London, and it was all man made. The aftershocks are going to be felt throughout the world, and there will be aftershocks aplenty."

Aftershock One

During 2000–2005, an average of 3,115 single-family homes were sold each year. For the year 2009, there will probably be only 2,190 sales, which means that there's been a decline of 30 percent. There were, on average, 2,494 condominium resales per year during that period, not including new-construction units. For 2009, I currently estimate that there will be about 1,735 condominium resales—a decline of 40 percent! (Note that new-construction sales are certainly adding to the number of transactions and are competing with the condominium resale market.)

Why?

Back in the good old days, a buyer could purchase a piece of San Francisco's expensive real estate with 5 percent down. Today's lenders require a minimum 20 percent down payment, which is a high hurdle for many people to clear.

Aftershock Two

It doesn't matter which pundit is right about when the economy will return to normal, because there is no normal to return to. Sorry, folks, besides predicting aftershocks, I forgot to make the point that the earthquake caused some deep fissures in the structure of the U.S. and California economies that are also impacting San Francisco real estate.

Washington is furiously printing money, which will lead to inflation. California and San Francisco are incurring major deficits that are likely to result in higher taxes and reduced services and will maybe cause fewer people to want the California experience. These combined factors are yet to be fully appreciated, even though San Francisco continues to enjoy more resilience than other parts of the country enjoy.

Aftershock Three

Now that the shaking has stopped and people are able to assess their personal damage, bargain hunters are out in force. In many instances, distressed properties are receiving multiple offers. Sure, they're at lower price levels, but it's a good sign that people are buying when they smell a bargain, and this is very encouraging for the entire market.

Aftershock Four

Thirty-year fixed rates can be had for under 5 percent right now. There is plenty of money available to grease the transaction; you just need to qualify for it. See aftershock one. A not insignificant problem, however, is that lenders are inundated with refinancing requests, so the refi process is taking longer than normal.

Aftershock Five

Transactions at the higher levels are down more than those at the lower levels for several reasons, the most important of which is that there are more lower-priced homes on the market, and more people are able to buy at the $750,000 level than at the $7.5 million level. That said, there is another reason: while a buyer may be willing and able to pay $7.5 million for a home, because the number of transactions at that price is way down, an appraisal may come in at $1.0 million short of that, and the deal may therefore get scuttled. Appraisers need comparable homes to justify an appraisal, and if they don't exist, the deal may not get done. While one might say that market value is determined by what buyers are willing to pay, the other part of the market includes the lenders who are party to the transaction. As a penance for their excesses, they are now being as conservative as they once were reckless, and if the only recent sales data that an appraiser has concerns short sales, that's the new market too.

Aftershock Six

Just as there was a big spike in the birthrate about nine months after the blackout in New York City in the mid-1960s, there will be a huge number of births in the next few years as a result of parents' not being able to afford evenings out. (I offer a disclaimer: I cannot prove this.) Of course, all of these future twenty- and thirtysomethings will have been fully indoctrinated by their parents about the perils of easy credit and hefty leverage. They will emerge between 2029 and 2039 to bail all of us out of this current financial mess. It takes a generation to forget the lessons of the previous one. So just think long term.

Summing Up

Though it will take time for the aftershocks to abate, demand-supply economics continues to prevail in San Francisco. No new single-family homes will be built (there's no land), and the construction of new condominiums has been throttled back until prices rise to justify the increased cost of construction. San Francisco residential real estate has been and will likely continue to be a profitable investment, but it is a long-term game.

It's about the Story
October 2009

Listen to my tale, and conjure up your own images. Interest rates are bumping along at historically all-time lows, and the prices of San Francisco residential real estate have dialed back to where they were four or more years ago. There's cheap money, and there are discounted prices on some of the best real estate in the world. A pretty good time to buy, right?

Many people—not all—are still afraid to buy. The best I can gather is that many are afraid to make a mistake, or they want to squeeze the seller as much as they can so that they feel that they've realized an absolute bargain.

The Media and Us

Yes, the Dow hit ten thousand, and Wall Street is all bubbly, but the media continues to focus on the 10 percent unemployment rate and the slowness of the eventual recovery.

I am not sure about this, but I would be willing to bet that the American media is the best at what it does. One of the things that it does so very well is disseminate stories worldwide very fast. Maybe there are parts of the world that didn't get the full dose of the dire economic story. Maybe some people are into living their own lives—damn the torpedoes, and full steam ahead.

That's an attitude that may be a perquisite for buying residential real estate amid the constant negative drumbeat of the media.

The San Francisco Story

So the real story, in my humble opinion, is that there are those who choose to live the life they want and those who live the life that others suggest for them. Given the drama and the economic inconsistencies that pass for news these days, it takes guts to pull the trigger, enter into a contract, and purchase a home, particularly for first-time buyers. And it's a gutsy move to pull the trigger when there's so much economic uncertainty all about us. Yes, you and I may have a good job today, but when we read about the 10 percent unemployment rate, we naturally pause, even when we're among the 90 percent who are employed.

While the majority on the sidelines think that they're watching the story play out and waiting for the game to change, thousands of others are writing their own stories. First-time buyers are purchasing their own home years before they ever thought they would. Buyers who were hoping to one day afford their dream house are now finding it more affordable than they'd ever imagined. Sellers who have owned their own home awhile are still able to sell at a profit and are able to scoop up a bargain when they buy a replacement property. Even sellers forced to sell at a loss are able to offset that loss with potential gains on the buy side.

It's more than figuring out how to make the numbers work. We are talking about people's homes and lives, not about pork bellies, stocks, or bonds. We are talking about choosing where and how you want to live life and then living it. So I will end my story with a quote by Buckminster Fuller, an inventor and a philosopher: "The minute you choose to do what you really want to do, it's a different kind of life."

Wealth and Power
December 2010

A couple of weeks ago, I attended a presentation about wealth creation.

Creating wealth is about accumulating assets, whether they are stocks, bonds, gold, rare coins, collectibles, or real estate. We know this, right?

Two things caught my attention. First, 46 percent of the billionaires listed by *Forbes* made their money in buying, selling, or developing real estate. Second, while I was attending a recent conference of financial CEOs in New York, as a group, they stated how positively they viewed real estate by saying, "Show us an asset that has been beaten up as much as real estate."

Where's the Power?

We got into trouble about five years ago, when people could get into real estate by putting effectively nothing down. The saying was, "Fog a mirror, and you can get a loan." If you buy an asset, *you need to invest in it.* In other words, you need to put enough down so that *you* have the *power.* Putting nothing down means that you effectively give the power to someone else—the lender. Ergo, the lender has the power to foreclose and throw you out. If you have the power, then you can decide if and when to sell. Real estate is not an asset that you can trade like a stock. You need to hold it for a period of time. Time, value, and money are the keys to creating wealth.

SINGLE-FAMILY HOMES VERSUS CONDOS NOVEMBER 2011

There are approximately ninety-five thousand single-family homes in the city, more than twice the estimated forty-three thousand condominiums.

From 1987 to 2000, the average single-family home sold at a 15 percent premium over the average price of a condominium. Starting in 2001, the single-family premium rose to 21 percent, and since 2003, the premium has jumped to a touch over 30 percent!

Get the Picture?

As you probably know, the inventory of single-family homes has remained the same in the last few decades. There just hasn't been any land to build on. On the other hand, condominium construction started booming in 2000, and although it has been dormant in the last few years, the inventory stock of condominiums increased by an estimated 25 percent since 2000.

Along with the growth in condominium units, the number of annual condominium resales has accelerated. It was a mere 899 in 1987, it peaked at 3,226 in 2004, and it's running at the rate of 2,200 in 2011.

Are Single-Family-Home Buyers Smarter?

The turnover rate in single-family inventory is about one-half the turnover rate of condominiums. Single-family buyers seem to be in for the longer haul; they typically stay in their home twice as long as condominium buyers do.

When it comes to selling, condominium owners appear to have a weaker negotiation position. More often than not, they accept a price lower than the original asking price.

Conclusions?

Like the stock market, it is up and down, up and down. It's difficult to discern any trends. Are we at a bottom? Is there going to be another price dip? No one really knows.

The best that buyers and sellers can do is recognize that the market is chaotic and try to find comfort by making long-term decisions with as much information as possible.

Have We Hit Bottom Yet? February 2012

We all know that the economy and real estate are cyclical. The last few years have witnessed a sizable downturn. Prices peaked in 2007, and since then, they've declined some 15 to 20 percent throughout the city.

The stock market has rallied to a high in early February 2012 not seen since May 2008. It reached a record 14,164 in October 2007.

National unemployment was 8.3 percent in January 2012, the lowest since February 2009, as shown below. San Francisco's unemployment dropped to 7.6 percent in January 2012, versus 11.1 percent for all of California.

New-product inventory south of Market Street is relatively miniscule, and there are about 450 unsold units: 140 at the Millennium, 260 at Madrone, and 50 at One Hawthorne. There is little resale inventory—just ask a real estate agent.

Recent IPOs, not to mention the fact that Facebook is in the wings, are creating more wealth.

Getting Back to Normal

"Normal" here is when people are buying and selling homes without being concerned that a trapdoor could open beneath them at any moment. Imagine what it was like for folks post-Depression as they tried to figure out whether life would get back to normal. What we just experienced was the greatest recession since the Great Depression. The American economy did not fully recover from the Great Depression until the Second World War effort started taking hold, and U.S. industry flexed its muscles.

We have been fighting two wars for ten years. New manufacturing jobs will not bring the economy back, but the American image will. The United States remains a mecca for people from throughout the world, and the wealthy from India, China, Brazil, Russia, and the Middle East still want to educate their children here, start a new business here, and buy real estate here. New York City and San Francisco beckon to them. Both are vibrant and have scores of young talent and a restricted residential supply.

There will be *no* announcement saying, "It's ok to get back in the market, and you will not get hurt." Meanwhile, there are many buyers in San Francisco writing offers and often competing. Many agents see properties come to market appropriately priced and enter into contract in days rather than weeks or months. Some sellers, however, cannot seem to bring themselves to part with their home at a price that does not reflect the "true value of their home." I still have not figured out what that really means. The market speaks loudly about market value.

Hit Bottom Yet?

Yes. Next question?

Where's the Supply?
March 2012

San Francisco buyers are out and about in great numbers. Engage an agent in conversation, and he or she will tell you that there's a lack of inventory. The Super Bowl has come and gone! It's spring already, and a dearth of inventory persists.

If we want to know why—which is always a fruitless exercise, as my college philosophy professor informed me—there are only two answers: "because" and "why not?" Rather than knowing why, maybe it's better to look at the traditional sources of supply and to think about the future.

I did some in-office research. I asked some fellow agents for the reason that their most recent seller sold. Here are the reasons in no particular order along with some editorial comments.

Divorce and Marriage

It seems that over the last few years, the divorce rate has actually declined in some forty-four of the fifty states. While that's good for the institution of matrimony, it is lousy for real estate agents and would-be buyers. Anecdotally, some couples stayed together to weather the recent recession and to avoid adding more economic hardship from a divorce. Now that the economy is on the rebound, perhaps we will see an uptick in divorces.

Living Longer

People are living longer; again, that's good for those who are doing the living, but it's not good for our real estate market. The life expectancy in San Francisco is high compared to the average life expectancy in the United States. San Francisco's death rates are lower than those of California and lower than those of Alameda and Contra Costa counties, but they're higher than those of Marin, San Mateo, and Santa Clara counties. Better health and aging of the population appear to be long-term trends, so there's no expected inventory here.

Had a Baby and Need More Room

We have a chance here. For as long as San Francisco remains a vibrant tech hotbed, it will continue to attract the young and eager, and they will do what they do, which is sell a place to move in with someone else and/or have a baby, need more room, and sell the one-bedroom to buy a two-or-more-bedroom home. Either way, more supply will be the result.

Relocation

When the great recession hit, major corporations put the brakes on relocation. Potential sellers stayed put. Now that the recession is thawing, corporations are easing back on the brakes, and some supply will likely flow. It is hard to say whether this will produce any meaningful supply.

New Construction

New construction south of Market ground to a halt once the recession hit. The Millennium, One Hawthorne, and Madrone are the only large developments with available inventory. There are a number of new developments planned for south of Market, but these will take several years to complete.

With the exception of the Van Ness corridor, only relatively small buildings can be built north of Market, given the forty-foot height limit, and they'll make a very little dent in the overall supply picture.

Rising Prices and the Future

Some would-be sellers have stayed put because they couldn't get the desired price for their home. Soon, prices will rise, which will likely generate more supply in the process.

Between 1998 and 2000 and between 2003 and 2005, average prices shot up by an average of more than 12 percent per year. Then we lost some 20 percent in overall value between 2008 and 2010. I regret to say that in the short term, meaningful supply does not seem to be in the cards, and quality-of-life issues in other parts of the world, particularly in China, will likely contribute to even more demand. How do you make your way through this thicket?

Thoughts on San Francisco Parking March 2013

Setting the Stage

Let's assume that you're thinking about buying a condominium, and let's exclude luxury buyers ($2 million or more) from the conversation. If you have a precious car, you need to park it somewhere, right?

Does it make sense to spend between $50,000 and $100,000 for a parking space, a cost that's usually included in the condominium price?

City Strategy

The city is focused on reducing the number of cars. There are various strategies. A transit-first approach and fewer cars are top priorities. They are increasing the number of bike lanes; employing articulated buses; and increasing the cost of parking meters, tickets, and neighborhood parking permits. From time to time, they even float the idea of congestion pricing, which would impose a fee on a trip from your home to downtown.

Does a Parking Space Appreciate?

Probably not, and certainly not at the same rate as actual living space. With an eight-by-sixteen foot parking space (128 square feet) and a cost of $75,000, one is paying $585 per square foot. While the city is making parking more expensive, car-sharing programs are making it easier to not own a car. When I lived in New York and housed my car in a garage (at a cost equal to another bedroom), my primary reason for having a car was to escape the city on the weekend. Weekend car rentals are a lot more expensive in New York than in San Francisco, and there are probably fewer reasons to escape San Francisco on the weekend.

Is It Easier to Sell a Condominium with Deeded Parking?

The answer is probably yes. However, the ease of selling is highly dependent on market conditions and location. When there is an abundance of buyers exceeding the available supply of property, as we have today, the issue of parking is far less of a decider than it is when markets are more evenly balanced between supply and demand.

In Summary

Ten years ago, I would have said, "Don't buy a condominium without a deeded parking space." Now I am less certain. The city is intent on reducing the number of cars and on making car ownership more expensive. In response, car-sharing programs are flowering. If you have ample financial resources, buy the parking space. Make sure that you inspect it first to assure that your car fits. If you're a couple with young kids, all bets are off. You need to own a car.

Comps
November 2013

The wrong question is, what is my property worth? The right question is, how much can I get for my property?

No one knows what a property is worth until the market speaks, and if one relies on comps for the answer, then one's thinking is limited. When I list properties, I always ask my sellers, what would you like and/or expect? More importantly, I ask myself what I can produce.

Comps

It's not that I don't like comps (I use them all the time); it's that they should not be used to determine what a property can sell for. Comps only get you into the ballpark. That's it. They're similar to a company's last profit-and-loss statement. That's history!

They tell you neither what buyers are thinking nor the state of the market nor what sale prices will be next week. They should not be used to determine what a seller *can* get for his or her property.

A few months ago, I received a call from an owner of a one-bedroom, one-bath 795-square-foot single-family home in Bernal Heights. The owners had lived it in for thirty-five years. A few colleagues advised me that it would sell for no more than $800,000 based on neighborhood comps. Instead of staging it, as was suggested by my sellers and colleagues, I lobbied to spend the same amount of money on architectural "drawings" (not plans) to understand what could be (which was a three-bedroom, two-and-a-half-bathroom 2,500-square-foot home that could sell at $2.5 million or more). We sold the property for $1.1 million.

In a Rising Market

Just like sellers, buyers use comps when they're searching for a property and thinking about making an offer. Successful buyers go beyond the comps.

I wouldn't call it genius, but I would submit that it takes original thinking to *maximize* a seller's return, rather than relying on comps and allowing market forces to do their thing. Instead of settling for a "good price," sellers can make some good money with an imaginative selling strategy. See the previous example.

List Price
June 2014

It's not easy for sellers and their agents to determine a good list price. Sellers generally want only one thing: the highest sale price. How to get there? That's the conundrum.

First, I believe in the real estate adage that you can't set a list price too low—the market will work its magic, and the true sale price will emerge. On the other hand, you can set it too high, and if buyers don't respond, you'll then need to lower it and suffer the likelihood that the property will be "tainted"—that is, the property will go into contract at an even lower price.

The Buy Side

I recently represented buyers looking for a property. They had a target price of not more than $800,000.

So we set up an MLS search with a price range of between $650,000 and $800,000. We looked at a lot of properties in many neighborhoods, and we finally wrote an offer at $825,000 for a property listed for $749,000.

We were in competition with three other buyers and eventually won the property with a price a touch over $900,000, a cool $100,000 more than they'd originally intended to spend.

Here's the point: had the agent listed the property closer to the ultimate contract price—say, at $899,000—my buyers would have never seen the property! My buyers didn't know that they would ultimately pay $100,000 more than they'd intended to pay, but they did.

Rationale

We hear that low interest rates are one of the reasons for our hypermarket. I agree. With interest rates this low, my buyers were able to afford principal and interest payments at the $900,000 level even though they'd thought that they could only afford payments at a much lower level.

No Benefit in Being Right

There's really not any benefit to setting a list price closer to what the agent may think will be the ultimate selling price. Who wins? No one. Fewer buyers will view the property at the higher price, and the seller will receive fewer offers, though the agent will perhaps do more work fielding calls and receiving more offers (too bad for the agent).

The One-More-Thing Bank
August 2014

The same week that one of the nation's major banks settled its federal lawsuit over bad mortgages for $7 billion, I had the unwelcome experience of meeting the same bank head on.

OMG! "Just one more thing" became the refrain ad nauseam. Let me briefly explain.

I listed a condominium in Lone Mountain and received and accepted a very nice offer from a very nice couple; it was their first property purchase (little did they know what was coming).

The bank's preapproval letter accompanied their offer; the buyers were *preapproved* and were putting down a hefty 40 percent. The deal was to close in twenty-six days, which is certainly a comfortable period for most San Francisco banks. Two days after the offer was accepted, the appraiser did his job and sent off an appraisal to the bank—so far, so good.

One of the buyers worked for a major accounting firm that had a "favorable financing" arrangement for its employees who used this bank for their residential financing needs.

Even though the bank had told the buyers that they were preapproved, the bank's ensuing actions spoke volumes and made it clear that that was not the case.

Of note are the facts that the loan officer was in Saint Louis, Missouri, and the underwriter was in Jacksonville, Florida. The wheels of this remotely located mortgage team moved at a snail's pace.

At one point, the buyers' agent reported to me that one of the buyers was in tears! Why? The bank needed just one more thing. This one-more-thing mantra continued. Of course, they missed the contract closing date.

My credo for buyers and sellers:

- Do not use a bank because your corporation has a "special" relationship with it.
- Do not use a bank whose loan officer, underwriter, or processing department is unfamiliar with the local lay of the land—that is, is located outside of California.
- If a bank provides a preapproval letter, all parties need to confirm that the underwriter has really done the preapproval work.

As in baseball, there's no crying in real estate—unless, of course, your bank has you in a vice and demands just one more thing.

Cars to the Slow Lane
November 2014

One of the propositions on our November ballot is Proposition A, which is ostensibly a $500 million bond measure to fix roads. As Phil Matier and Andrew Ross opined recently, it is "really the first step in a master plan to put buses, bikes, and pedestrians on the fast track and move cars into the slow lane."

The proposition includes $142 million for new traffic signals, crosswalks, and other projects to speed Muni and to make it safer to cross the street and $52 million to build thirty-five miles of new bike lanes, plus more red-bus-only lanes. As such, there will be less room for car lanes.

No Surprise

This should not come as any surprise. The city is, and has been for some time, intent on reducing the number of cars on our streets. You've noticed that parking meters and parking tickets cost more, residential parking permits cost more, and the number of parking spaces is being reduced, right?

So What?

I am trying to figure out what this means for the value of deeded parking spaces. I am not at all sure.

On the one hand, the need for a car is reduced now that we have car-share companies like Uber and Lyft and, theoretically, better Muni service, all of which enable people to get around easier, as the city fathers intended. Thus, there is or will be less need and less demand for deeded parking spaces—but not from parents with school-aged children.

On the other hand, our San Francisco population is growing, and the affluence of that population is increasing, both of which will increase the demand side of the equation.

While a few parking spaces have traded for more than $100,000 and some developers price new spaces for $45,000, the average value of a deeded parking space is roughly $75,000. My car costs me at least $5,000 a year for gas, parking, insurance, and repairs, not to mention depreciation or lease payments. That represents a lot of Uber, taxis, and car sharing.

This is our future, folks. We might as well get used to it.

2015 Predictions
January 2015

The Giants will not be World Series champs in 2015. How do I know? Well, 2015 is an odd year, and they no longer have the Panda.

Demand

As of December 2014, there were 7.3 billion people in the world, and they all wanted to live in San Francisco. How do I know? (I really don't.) And in December 2013, there were only 7.1 billion people in the world, and I just think that if they could have swung it, they all would have liked to live in San Francisco. Anyone think I'm wrong?

Prices

The average condominium sales price per square foot in South Beach and Yerba Buena will exceed the average condominium sales price per square foot in the traditionally most expensive neighborhoods of Presidio Heights, Pacific Heights, Cow Hollow, and the Marina. How do I know? It already does.

Average prices for both single-family homes and condominiums will appreciate some 10 percent in 2015 (over 2014 prices). How do I know? Because my crystal ball says that 2015 is the fourth inning of a seven-inning housing up cycle in San Francisco.

Automobiles

With the exception of gasoline prices, everything associated with owning an automobile in the city will continue to escalate. How do I know? The city government's long-term policy is to reduce the number of cars in the city, so it will continue to increase the price of parking meters, parking tickets, residential parking fees, and so on, thus making alternate forms of transportation more attractive.

San Francisco's high-rise office and residential developers will complain to Mayor Lee about downtown automobile congestion. How do I know? Because they complained in 2014 while forgetting that they were the ones responsible for the ongoing construction that screwed up normal traffic flow.

Owning Something or Not
June 2015

A recent op-ed piece by Thomas Friedman in the *New York Times* caught my eye and taught me the following facts:

- Uber, the world's largest taxi company, owns no vehicles.
- Facebook, the world's most popular media owner, creates no content.
- Alibaba, the most valuable retailer, has no inventory.
- Airbnb, the world's largest accommodation provider, owns no real estate.

(Wow, I had never thought about it in that context!)

Friedman goes on to say that "we're at the start of a major shift on the question of what's worth owning."

I think that that's a very interesting, conceptual, financial, existential question.

Two-thirds of the San Francisco population rent rather than own, either because they can't afford to own, they don't plan to be here for very long, or they just prefer to leave ownership headaches to someone else.

For the other one-third, owning one's home is conceptually, financially, and existentially a good thing. I'm no expert regarding the conceptual or existential issues, and I need not be a financial expert to appreciate what is happening in San Francisco.

Average prices continue to escalate in 2015 (they're up more than 10 percent so far this year), and this is after they increased 12 percent per year in 2012, 2013, and 2014. If you're not in the game, you need to get in the game; do whatever it takes.

Credits:

San Francisco Maps
Bart Wright, Fine Line Maps
Oakland, California

Photos of Cover Image and High-Rise Buildings
Dan Freidman Photography
San Francisco, California

www.ingramcontent.com/pod-product-compliance
Lightning Source LLC
Chambersburg PA
CBHW071813200526
45169CB00017B/215
9781523952748